The Lucky Drinker Cocktail Book

unforgettable drinks with a modern approach

Ciprian Zsraga

Photography by Tom Elms

Clink Street

Published by Clink Street Publishing 2021

ISBN:
978-1-913962-70-8 - paperback
978-1-913962-71-5 - ebook

Contents

Introduction

This book represents a journey in the world of cocktails from a historic point of view and in addition, treats deeply various aspects: from basic bar techniques to advanced innovative ideas that can be used to create impressive drinks (such as pressure infusion, clarification, smoking, aging, fermentation, clarification and even spherification that is still seen as a taboo in the bar industry nowadays).

Bar equipment, ice, bar personalities and how they influence the world, what are the elements and what is the approach to create an outstanding cocktail, food and beverage pairing, alcohol intake but also how to calculate the cost of a cocktail: very important aspects that will help you to have a profitable cocktail menu.

In addition, there is a section dedicated to the bar equipment, bar personalities who shape the bar industry, bar tales and 'gigy' facts, and much much more.

It is vital to possess the knowledge, and it can be acquired through education and experience: through theoretical information and practical understanding of a subject.

As for the theoretical information, this concept is explained better on the next pages: have patience and read very carefully and even more important, in order to understand the concept of the topics, put into practice what you will learn here.

My name is Ciprian Zsraga and I love to describe bartending as an art. For sure is not an easy one and the bartender is not just someone that place 'stuff' in a shaker and serve it but also must be a psychologist, multilanguage speaker, doctor and above all must be a master of hospitality.

It needs time and patience to master this skill but remember that the hospitality started when we born: food, drink, smile and a hug, this is what made us happy as kids and it stays for the rest of our life, and this is what we are looking for when we walk in a bar. This 'skill' cannot be translated into words because it comes from within you and must be done with the heart!

I've been part of the hospitality industry since a very young age. In 2006 after attending the Hospitality Institute in the South of Italy and after covering different roles in the hospitality sector there, I decided to move to London, where I had the opportunity to work alongside bartender gurus from whom I learned and mastered bar and knowledge skills, working in magic places voted various times best bars in the world during annual international competitions, bars that are every bartender dream to work in, such as Artesian bar at the Langham Hotel and American bar at the Savoy.

There has always been a passion for writing and the idea started in 2017 as a blog with the aim to inspire, educate and spread love and passion for the bar sector, and since its foundation, the pillars have always been the same: 'drink quality, drink in company and above all drink responsibly!'.

Now is time to distil my philosophy but also to bring a pinch of innovation and knowledge into the bar industry by creating this book and share worldwide with all of you.

Enjoy!

Bar personalities

Here is a list of the most notorious bar personalities who shaped and continue sculpting the bar industry, and keep in mind that this list does not include the superb work done by many brand ambassadors, owners, founders, bartenders, as will be way too long but a special thank you goes to them as well.

Jerry Thomas

We have to start this chapter with Jerry Thomas aka 'The Professor', and the reason is that he gave birth to the first cocktail book in the world, *How to Mix Drinks or the Bon Vivant's Companion*, published in 1862.

Many of the drinks presented in his book are still in circulation today and many of the cocktails in those days created are still inspired by the drinks there present.

He was very well known also for his skills, especially when making the Blue Blazer cocktail, a mixture that consists of sugar, water, and whiskey that was set on fire and using two silver mixing cups, the fired drink was thrown from one cup to another creating a spectacular arc of fire before being served in a tumbler.

Harry Johnson

Harry Johnson is another precursor of the bar industry alongside his rival Jerry Thomas. By Russian roots, he moved to the US where started to work as a kitchen boy and progressing until later he opened and owned different bars across the US and also opened the first bar consulting agency in 1890.

Very well known for his 1882 *Bartender's Manual* as being the first bar book containing information on cocktails but also management information on how to run a bar.

Harry Craddock

The author of the *Savoy Cocktail Book*, first published in 1930 and in print since then, definitely influenced the bar industry, and it still continues with his work as this book is a must-have for all the bartenders across the globe. UK born, he moved to the US in 1897 and after working in some of the greatest establishments in that era there (Knickerbocker Hotel and Hoffman House) he moved back to London during Prohibition, to work at the American Bar at the Savoy Hotel, bringing American cocktail knowledge from across the ocean.

A mention goes also to the fact that he was the first president of the United Kingdom Bartenders Guild.

Ada Coleman

If we mention the American bar at the Savoy and Harry Craddock, we have to mention also Ada Coleman: very often cited as the only female head bartender in this iconic bar (although there are theories that there was another female head bartender before and during her time there). She worked there for 23 years before and together with Harry Craddock and during her time there she is credited with the birth of some iconic drinks – one of the most famous ones is the Hanky Panky.

Harry MacElhone

His name is associated with the famous New York Bar in Paris and his name is linked as being the father of some of the most iconic drinks in circulation today: French 75, Bloody Mary, Sidecar, Monkey Gland and Boulevardier. Some theories say he is the creator of the White Lady cocktail while working at the Savoy hotel in London, but others say he started designing this drink while at Ciro's Club using gin, mint liqueur, triple sec and lemon juice. During his time here, published a book *Harry of Ciro's ABC of Mixing Cocktails* in 1921 and from here on he became a celebrity.

Hugo Ensslin

German roots but often associated with the US as in 1917 he published the *Recipes for Mixed Drinks*, being the last cocktail book to be published before Prohibition. The very interesting story regards the Aviation cocktail – as he is the creator, but people for many years preferred the recipe from the more famous *Savoy Cocktail Book* – is that when Harry Craddock copied Ensslin's recipe to be featured in his book he forgot apparently to insert the Violette liqueur, key ingredient when making this drink as the colour is reminiscent of the blue sky as the drink has been created in honour of WW1 British pilots.

Don Beach

The person that has the most notoriety as being the pioneer of the tiki movement is Ernest Raymond Beaumont-Gantt, known as Don Beach after he opened Don the Beachcomber restaurant in Los Angeles in 1934 as the first tiki style. Author of a vast amount of tiki cocktails and one of them that is still popular today is the Zombie cocktail.

Victor Bergeron

Also known as Trader Vic's and his name is associated with Polynesian-themed in the bar and restaurant industry. He is the author of many successful tiki cocktail books but also of very successful themed restaurants as franchising, spreading more than 20 across the globe. His name is also linked as being one of the creators of the Mai Tai cocktail, together with Don Beach.

Constate Ribalaigua

Barcelona born and Cuban emigrated with his family, where he started and developed a passion for the bar industry since young age. He started in the bar business and later he owned a bar called El Floridita that was hugely frequented by Americans during Prohibition.

Ernest Hemingway frequented this bar and later became his favourite bar. He even mentioned it several times in his books. Constate created a drink for the American author and name it Papa Doble, as Ernest was known as Papa and doble because the drink contained a double measure of rum.

With his delicious creations he gained the name 'El Rey de los Cocteleros' (The King of Cocktails).

Ian Fleming

Not a bartender but through his James Bond novels, he universalized cocktails worldwide in particular the famous 'shaken not stirred' Vesper Martini, which is still popular and hugely requests worldwide.

David Embury

Another non-bartender, Embury was an American tax lawyer with such a huge understanding and passion for mixing drinks that in 1948 he published the encyclopaedic *The Fine Art of Mixing Drink*, a work that today is appreciated but also opinionated.

Gary (Gaz) Regan

British born but moved to the US where he started the bar career. Author of more than 18 books on cocktails and bartending aspects. Very famous for wearing eyeliner under one of his eyes and the reason was "to remind bartenders that the eye contact with customers is vital."

In 2018 he launched the Worldwide Bartender Database, an online portal for bartenders and spirits producers with the aim to educate, career enhancement, and the opportunity to work with brands.

Dick Bradsell

He is the creator of some of the most consumed drinks worldwide and in particular the Espresso Martini, Bramble, and Russian Spring Punch. Part of London's bartender scene which he influenced in the 90s and 2000s.

Sasha Petraske

The founder of a highly acclaimed speakeasy themed Milk and Honey bar in New York but also many other bars across the globe, he has been very influential in the bar industry in modern times. Sadly, he passed away at a young age: 42 years old, but his legacy continues.

Ted Haigh

Nicknamed 'Dr Cocktail', he is linked with the bar history through his historian work and a book that marked many bartenders' grown, Haig published in 2004: *Vintage Spirits and Forgotten Cocktails*, bringing to modern days the buried world of cocktails.

Jeff Berry

Nowadays the major exponent of tiki culture is Jeff 'Beachbum' Berry. He expresses the love for Polynesian philosophy through various books and cocktails on the subject, but also through many seminars worldwide.

Robert Hess

The co-founder of the Museum of the American Cocktail, Robert Hess used his passion and expertise to educate the bartenders by publishing articles, books, videos, blogs, conducting seminars, and many more.

Salvatore Calabrese

Known as 'The Maestro' with over 50 years of a distinguished career in the bar industry. Author of more than ten bar books, liqueurs, bar equipment, cocktails as well as cocktails challenge creator (The Maestro Challenge); all this known worldwide. His name is also associated with serving tv personalities and royals but also linked with the Guinness World Record as he created in 2012 the Salvatore's Legacy cocktail, using a mix of a total of 770 years of liquid history for a value of £5500 per drink sold, with the drink being composed of 40ml of 1788 Clos de Griffier Vieux Cognac, 20ml of 1770 Kummel Liqueur, 20ml of 1860 Dubb Orange Curaçao and two dashes of Angostura bitters from the 1900s.

Peter Dorelli

Another living legend and same as Salvatore Calabrese with over 50 years of bar experience. His name is associated with the American Bar at the Savoy, being there for many years, training under Joe Gilmore, until later becoming himself Head Bartender until 2003 when he retired at the age of 63 years. And since the retirement, his role across the globe has been fundamental for the younger generation of bartenders as he dedicated his time to educate and inspire.

Alessandro Palazzi and Agostino Perrone

Some of the best Martinis in the world are served in London and on the podium, we have the Dukes bar where the legendary Alessandro Palazzi often called the Kind of the Martinis, delights you with cold Martinis and amazing tales.

Agostino Perrone and its team at the Connaught bar will make you live a memorable experience through the art of hospitality and absolutely excellent service while serving you truly world-class tailored Martinis and other delicious cocktails.

Dale DeGroff

One of the most iconic bar personalities in the US, known as 'King Cocktail', had and continues to have a huge and successful impact in educating and spreading passion for this craft. He is also the founding president of Museum of the American Cocktail. He improved the recipe of the Cosmopolitan cocktail and made it popular.

Audrey Saunders

After attending a seminar with Dale DeGroff, in 1996 Audrey decides to make her way into the bar industry and many years afterward she opened the Pegu Club bar in the US, putting into practice her vision on the craft. Nowadays is often referred to her as one of the very best bartenders, she is credited with the invention of worldwide known modern cocktails such as Old Cuban and Gin Gin Mule.

Kazuo Uyeda

Owner of the acclaimed Tender bar, based in Japan, Kazuo Uyeda started bartending in the 60s and his name is associated with the hard shake and the philosophy behind it. Author of several books and winner of the various cocktail competition, he earned a reputation as the best bartender in the Japanese scene.

David Wondrich

The author of one of some of the very best books on drinks from a historic perspective, *Imbibe!* and *Punch*, and endless articles, David Wondrich gained a lot of notoriety through his research and education seminars that he still doing these days.

Jared Brown and Anastasia Miller

Authors of more than 30 books including *Shaken Not Stirred: A Celebration of the Martini*, *Champagne Cocktails*, *Cuba: Legend of Rum*, *The Soul of Brasil*, *Spirituous Journey: A History of Drink*, *The Mixellany Guide to Vermouth and Other Aperitifs*, winners of many accolades, this duo are conducting research that dated back millennia on the subject. Jared Brown and Anastasia Miller have changed the bar industry's face through their work and continue to inspire a generation of bartenders.

Marian Beke

Slovakian-born moved to London and after working in some iconic places (Townhouse, Montgomery Place, Artesian, Purl) he joined a new project at Nightjar. Globally acclaimed him and the bar, after five years working there, in 2015 Marian opened his own place in London, the Gibson bar and only after few weeks from the opening, the bar has been listed number 6 at the World's 50 Best Bars. A very unique style of drinks and perhaps the most innovative mind in present days.

Alex Kratena and Simone Caporale

Every modern bartender knows this duo and how they influenced and still do the bar scene. Gained a lot of popularity while working at the Artesian bar at The Langham Hotel in London, ranked best bar in the world four times in a row. Their unique approach to drinks consists of phenomenal serving, exceptional hospitality, and what was unique is the fact that they broke the barrier of the hotel bar and reimagined it. Now Alex has opened his bar in London with his partner, another influential bartender, Monica Berg, and Simone his bar in Barcelona, but they are still traveling to educate and inspire bartenders worldwide.

Erik Lorincz

Another influential bar personality who inspires and educates bartenders across the globe and truly an example to follow: from barback in Slovakia to head bartender of the most iconic hotel bar in the world, to owner. In 2010 he was crowned as Bartender of the Year during the World Class competition and soon afterward joined the American Bar at the Savoy as the tenth head bartender and during his time there, the bar has been awarded the best bar in the world.

Ryan Chetiyawardana

One of the very innovative bartenders in circulation: the mind behind Dandelyan bar rated as the best bar in the world a few years ago. Using his background in philosophy, biology, and art he created an innovative vision on drinks that he is applying to his bars around the world, but also sharing them through his seminars, videos, articles, etc.

Major actors of alcohol globalization

Ten major actors of alcohol globalization and some of the brands that they own and/or produce:

Diageo
Gin: Tanqueray, Gordon's, Jinzu.
Vodka: Ketel One, Smirnoff, Cîroc.
Rum: Ron Zacapa, Captain Morgan.
Tequila: Don Julio, Casamigos.
Whisk(e)y: Johnnie Walker, Crown Royal, Haig Club, Seagram's, George Dickel, Talisker, Lagavulin, Caol Ila, Oban, J&B, Bell's, Buchanan's, Cardhu, Bulleit, Roe and Co.
Liqueur: Baileys, Pimm's. Beer: Guinness.

Pernod Ricard
Gin: Beefeater, Plymouth.
Vodka: Absolut, Luksusowa.
Rum: Havana Club, Malibu.
Tequila: Avion, Olmeca Altos
Brandy: Martell.
Whisk(e)y: Chivas Regal, Jameson, Red Breast, The Glenlivet, Ballantine's.
Other: Kahlúa, Ricard, Mumm and Perrier – Jouet champagne,

Beam Suntory
Gin: Larios, Sipsmith, Roku.
Vodka: Haku, Pinnacle.
Rum: Cruzan
Tequila: Sauza.
Brandy: Courvoisier.
Whisk(e)y: Jim Beam, Maker's Mark, Canadian Club, Knob Creek, Teacher's, Laphroaig, Bowmore, Auchentoshan, the Ardmore, Connemara, Canadian Club, Hakushu, Hibiki, Yamazaki.

Bacardi Limited
Gin: Bombay
Vodka: Grey Goose, Eristoff
Rum: Bacardi, Banks, Santa Teresa
Tequila: Patrón, Cazadores.
Brandy: Baron Otard, D'USSÉ
Whisk(e)y: Dewar's, William Lawson's, Aberfeldy, Aultmore, Royal Brackla, Craigellachie, Angel's Envy
Other: Martini, Noilly Prat, St-Germain, Bénédictine, Drambuie, Leblon.

Brown Forman
Gin: Fords
Vodka: Finlandia
Tequila: Herradura, El Jimador
Whisk(e)y: Jack Daniel's, Woodford Reserve, Old Forester, Canadian Mist.
Other: Chambord

LVMH
Brandy: Hennessy
Vodka: Belvedere
Whisk(e)y: Ardbeg, Glenmorangie.
Other: Dom Pérignon, Moët & Chandon, Krug, Veuve Clicquot, Ruinart, Grand Marnier.

Campari Group
Gin: Bulldog, Ondina.
Vodka: Skyy
Rum: Appleton Estate, Wray and Nephew, Trois Rivières.
Mezcal: Montelobos
Whisk(e)y: Wild Turkey, Russell's Reserve, Glen Grant, Old Smuggler
Other: Campari, Aperol, Cynar, Cinzano, Frangelico, Averna, Grand Marnier,

William Grant and Sons
Gin: Hendrick's
Vodka: Reyka, Russian Standard.
Rum: Sailor Jerry
Whisk(e)y: Glenfiddich, Grant's, The Balvenie, Monkey Shoulder, Tullamore DEW
Other: Drambuie, Ancho Reyes.

Edrington Group
Rum: Brugal
Vodka: Snow Leopard
Whisk(e)y: The Macallan, Highland Park, The Famous Grouse, Cutty Sark

Rémy Cointreau
Gin: The Botanist
Rum: Mount Gay
Brandy: Rémy Martin, Metaxa.
Whisk(e)y: Bruichladdich
Other: Cointreau, Passoã.

Bar Equipment

Let's make some drinks but before that please allowed me to introduce you to some bar equipment and techniques.

Shaker

It is an essential tool that is used to mix liquids that have different densities by shaking, and the aim is also to bring the temperature down and to incorporate vital dilution to the final result.

I prefer metal as a material for the shaker because it has a lower temperature compared to that of glass. So, the thermal mass is excellent and as they are also lighter, they need less energy to cool the drinks and you have also more control for the dilution; plus, they also have a longer-term duration.

They come in different sizes and shapes. Here are the most common examples:

- Boston Shaker consisting of two pieces, the bottom is metal, and the top can be glass or metal.
- The Cobbler Shaker: also known as the three-piece shaker and the great aspect is that has a strainer incorporated. When used correctly with the shaking technique with the cobbler, the result is a magnificent show to see, plus positive effects on the cocktail.
- The French Shaker also known as Parisienne, consists of a two-piece shaker with a metal bottom and a metal cap.

The **mixing glass** is a glass-like container, used together with a bar spoon and a strainer for the preparation of cocktails with the stir & strain technique. The mixing glass allows you to cool the drinks without watering them down. It is suitable for mixing those cocktails which, containing particularly delicate ingredients such as distilled spirits, wines, and liqueurs (defined in jargon 'clear') that must be simply mixed and not shaken with the shaker.

A **bar spoon** is a long-handled spoon used in bartending principally for mixing drinks with the stirring technique. It can be also used for layering of both alcoholic and non-alcoholic mixed drinks, garnish, and even to muddle (but this depends on its shape). Its length ensures that it can reach the bottom of the tallest jug or tumbler to mix ingredients directly in the glass.

A bar spoon holds about 5 millilitres of liquid (the same as a conventional teaspoon). Its long handle is usually decorative and elegant – some variations mimic large swizzle sticks, with a disc at one end. The shaft is typically thin and threaded so that the fingers can easily grip and rotate the spoon.

The **strainer** is a metal bar accessory used to separate ice from a mixed drink when is poured into the serving glass. It is used by placing it over the mouth of the glass or shaker in which the beverage was prepared and pour; the small holes in the device allow only liquids to pass as the beverage is poured.

There are the most common types of strainers.

- The Hawthorne strainer is a disc (called 'rim') with a handle and two or more stabilizing prongs. A metal spring fixed around the edge of the rim rolls inward to fit inside the glass or the shaker and allowed out only the liquid.
- The Julep strainer is shaped like a bowl with a handle and will fit tightly into a mixing glass or shaker when inserted at the proper angle. Liquid passes through holes.

- Fine mesh strainer is used when need to *double strain* the drink as is designed to stop any fine, unwanted particles from falling into the drink such as ice shards, fruit, seeds etc.

Jigger is used to measure the volume.

Even if you use the jigger when preparing a cocktail always taste the drinks before pouring them into the serving vessels as at this stage you can still correct it in case you are not happy with the result.

A **muddler** is a bartender's tool, used like a pestle to muddle fruits, herbs, and spices in the bottom of a glass/shaker to release their flavour. Can be wood or plastic. The second one is preferably more because the wood tends to keep the smell of the previous muddle cocktail even after being washed. One of the best muddle drink examples is a Mojito.

The **cutting board** allows you to chop fruits, herbs. A silicone cutting board is better because is durable, heat resistant, and non-slip; Easy to clean and doesn't keep bacteria.

The **knife** is a tool with a cutting edge or blade, hand-held or otherwise, with most having a different handle material. There are many styles and some types of knives are used as utensils and others are used in the ice's processing.

The **metal pour** is the instrument that if used correctly allows pouring the quantity of prefixed liquid with extreme precision. Made with a base of rubber to fit in the neck of bottles of spirits or liqueurs and a part in stainless steel with an air filter.

Tongs are a type of tool used to grip fruits, herbs, and everything that goes inside the drink or used as a garnish, instead of holding them directly with hands. There are many forms of tongs adapted to their specific use. Again, different sizes but the purpose is always the same.

Peeler. Useful not only to peel vegetables like potatoes and carrots or fruit but also to produce citrus peel to decorate your drink.

An **ice pick** is a tool used to break up or to model ice. Its shape resembles a scratch awl for wood. Before modern refrigerators, ice picks were a ubiquitous household tool used for separating and shaping the blocks of ice used in iceboxes. Easily chips and breaks up blocks of ice for use in all types of drinks.

Its role is to create ice chunks that melt slower than using ice cubes that normally melt quickly. You can prepare different shapes and sizes also with the help of other utensils (such as a knife).

Mexican elbow squeezer is one of the best squeezers in the business for juicing instantly various citrus fruits, such as oranges, lemons, and limes.

The mechanism of the Mexican elbow works on a hinge, simply lift the top arm of the squeezer, place your cut fruit into the bowl (with the skin or outer edge of the fruit facing upwards) and push the top arm back down, squeezing together both handles tightly to juice your fruit of choice.

So called because is related to the motion of how the squeezer works and because probably it was invented in Mexico.

The **swizzle stick** is normally a small wooden stick used in the preparation of the swizzle drinks. The original swizzle sticks were created in the 18th century at a plantation in the West Indies.

The **digital refractometer** is a portable, water-resistant measurer for determining the sugar content in a liquid with a measuring range of 0 to 85% brix. The measurement result is displayed in the large LCD display of the digital refractometer. Depending on the type of refractometer the measuring of sucrose, fructose, glucose or invert sugar is carried out quickly and easily.

Blender. Used for preparation that has more of a liquid consistency such as smoothies, milkshakes, frozen drinks but also sour drinks with egg white presence. Thanks to their tall, narrow jars and lids with a watertight seal, they can handle all those liquid ingredients.

The **portable smoking gun** adds a big, smoky flavour and aroma to foods and beverages in just a few seconds.

The smoking gun works with a variety of wood smoking chips, teas, and spices, even hay, dried flowers and herbs. To use, simply fill the gun chamber with desired combustibles, turn it on, light combustibles with a match or lighter. The flexible extender hose makes it easy to apply the smoke directly where it's wanted, even inside resealable bags and containers.

Fire torch is a precious little item for many chefs and bartenders, to create perfect finishing touches to a variety of different dishes, desserts, or used to add some world-class touches to your cocktail.

Soda siphons have been in use since the 1830s and were a mainstay of the speakeasy and jazz bar scene of the 1920s and 1930s. Give your bar a retro-chic vibe whilst producing sparkling, clear carbonated water on demand with a seltzer bottle-style siphon. Cocktail siphons utilize disposable CO2 canisters in order to complete cocktails with flair and fizz.

Cream whipper. Use the cream whipper to whip cream, ice cream, frostings, soft cheese, pastry cream, soda, jellies and a whole lot more.

Usually are made from high-grade brushed aluminium (last for years) and are antibacterial and easy to clean.

Works with N20 (Nitrous Oxide) cartridge and normally each cartridge holds 8 g of gas. Two cartridges are typically sufficient to charge a 1 L siphon.

Whipping siphons were designed for aerating creams high in fat. Nitrous oxide (NO2) dissolves much better in fat than in water, so high-fat liquids generally foam better in a siphon than low-fat ones do. You can, however, foam any liquid thick enough to hold bubbles. Add starch, gelatine, eggs, or agar to thin liquids to give them enough body for foaming.

Instant read thermometer. Use the thermometer to find out a drink's temperature in only few seconds. The idea is to serve the drink at its right temperature; there is nothing worse than a warm Martini.

Usually, it offers a temperature range from -49ºF to 392ºF or -45ºC to 200ºC. Stick probe into drink then read the temperature out from the digital LCD display.

The **AeroPress** is a revolutionary new way to make perfect coffee every time. It is really simple to use: gentle air pressure will create a coffee with a smooth rich flavour with lower acidity and without bitterness.

It was invented in 2005 by Aerobie president Alan Adler. The coffee is steeped for 10–50 seconds (depending on grind and preferred strength) and then forced through a filter by pressing the plunger through the tube. The filters used are either the AeroPress paper filters or disc-shaped thin metal filters.

The device consists of two nesting cylinders. One cylinder has a flexible airtight seal and fits inside the larger cylinder, similar to a syringe. The cylinders are moulded of polypropylene.

In addition can be used to make rapid infusion cocktails such as Coffee Negroni.

Drip cold machine. Another alternative way to produce coffee. It consists of heat-resistant glass, permanent filter mesh, a lid handle strainer frame made of polypropylene. Add the coffee grounds and 24 hours later enjoy an aromatic and delicious cold coffee.

Cold-brew is a super-slow method in which ground beans are steeped in room-temperature water for anything between 12 and 24 hours, drawing out different flavours to a hot brew.

The method consists of placing water in a top compartment, grinds in the middle with a valve leading to the bottom where your cold-brew drips through.

I recommend you to start with a 1:4 coffee to water ratio and then experimenting with different ratios to reach different strengths.

Once the coffee is done, you can store it in the fridge for up to a week, diluting, reheating, or serving chilled as you prefer.

The **French press** is a cylindrical pot with a plunger and built-in filter screen that presses hot water through ground coffee. The French press is used to create an earthy, rich coffee cup. The secret is all in the grind: choose medium, with uniformity and consistency throughout. Very coarse grinds may clog the filter, while very fine grinds will pass through the filter, muddying the results.

Ice cream machine. With the help of these machines, you don't have to be a culinary genius to create an exciting and delicious dessert or your favourite snack. A great idea is to use it in the cocktail making: olive ice cream to be served with your Martini, or perhaps a Negroni ice cream.

There is a huge range of ice-cream makers that will enable you to create not only ice cream but sorbet and frozen yogurt too. To make sorbet is a similar process as making ice cream but is made without milk and is made with fruit. Make sure that you transform the fruit into a puree before putting it into the ice cream machine.

Thermomix. Often called the world's most intelligent food processor, Thermomix lets you weigh, chop, blend, mix, grind, grate, cook, steam, whisk, knead and so much more all within one compact machine.

With Thermomix, you can regularly make all sorts of dairy-free alternatives that were previously unaffordable and that you never would have considered making at home. (Think almond milk, soy milk, oat milk, hemp milk, rice milk, and milk from quinoa, coconut, sunflower seeds, and other nuts!)

Air fryers are attractive for their convenience, safety, and health benefits. An air fryer is a kitchen appliance that cooks by circulating hot air around the food. A mechanical fan circulates the hot air around the food at high speed, cooking the food and producing a crispy layer via the Maillard effect.

Traditional frying methods induce the Maillard effect by completely submerging foods in hot oil. The air fryer works alternatively by coating the desired food while circulating air heated up to 200°C to confer energy and initiate the reaction. By doing this the appliance is able to fry foods like potato chips, chicken, fish, steak, French fries, or pastries while using between 70% and 80% less oil than a traditional deep-fryer.

Most air fryers come with adjustable temperature and timer knobs that allow for more precise cooking. Food is cooked in a cooking basket that sits atop a drip tray. The basket and its contents must be periodically shaken to ensure uniform cooking; some models accomplish this by incorporating a food agitator that continuously churns the food during the cooking process while others require the user to perform the task manually.

Grass juicer. If you want to add a healthy dose to your cocktails, then you will need wheatgrass juicers. Wheatgrass juicers are low speed or hand-cranked juicers that exert a high pressing force on this nutritious but tough ingredient. Wheatgrass has a relatively low juice yield, so you need to choose an efficient wheatgrass juicer.

Wheatgrass is the young grass of the common wheat plant called Triticum aestivum. This (gluten-free, of course!) edible grass is juiced into a 'wheatgrass shot', that can be consumed on its own, or used in combination with other juices to create a super healthy cocktail.

Centrifugal juicers. It is a very effective tool for filtering/separation by the use of gravity. A centrifuge uses rotational forces to separate food into layers by density.

It works by shredding ingredients using toothed blades on the bottom of a rapidly spinning sieve basket. The spinning force then separates the juice from the pulp, flinging the pulp into the pulp bin while the juice filters through to the container or jug. Centrifugal juicers often have different speeds and higher-end models sometimes include a 'soft fruit' disc too, allowing you to juice fruits such as berries, which centrifugal juicers are usually poor at juicing. Buying a more expensive model can mean you get a higher quality commercial-grade motor, more durable metal rather than plastic parts, and a longer warranty.

Vacuum packing is the process of extending the lifespan of food/drinks by removing air from the packaging. Commercially, professional kitchens use vac packing to prepare food in advance of service or for cooking using a sous vide machine.

Sous vide, which is French for 'under vacuum' is a method of cooking food sealed in airtight containers in a water bath. It was developed in France in the early 1970s when George Pralus and a food scientist joined forces to devise the perfect method for producing foie gras. After numerous experiments, the best method proved to be sealing the food in a pouch by using a vacuum packing machine before cooking it very slowly at a controlled temperature.

Food cooked in this way lasts longer than normal cooking times – 72 hours in some cases – at an accurately regulated temperature much lower than normally used for cooking, typically around 55°C to 60°C for meats and higher for vegetables. The intention is to cook the item evenly and to not overcook the outside while still keeping the inside at the same 'doneness', which keeps the food juicier.

Sous vide allows chefs and bartenders to maximize advance preparation. It also reduces wastage, making sous vide a highly cost-effective cooking method.

The **ice machine** is a useful device for producing ice. A mould is filled automatically with water (through a tube that connects it to the water system) and, after a few hours, the mould is turned upside down so that the ice cubes fall into the appropriate container. The cycle repeats until the container fills, then the ice will push on a special lever which will stop the production of ice until the container is emptied.

Rotary evaporation or rotavap is essentially a machine that vacuum distils and a very interesting fact is that no cuts is needed.

The vacuum lowers the boiling/evaporation temperature of the liquid, therefore allowing you to distil liquids at temperatures as low as 35°C. The rotating flask is there to increase surface area, therefore increasing the rate of evaporation.

Some coolness factors of the rotovap:

You are able to collect two liquids from it. One is the precipitate which is the clear liquid, and there's the concentrate which is in the rotating flask. The precipitate has the aromatics of the original liquid. Aromatics are usually volatile and will usually be carried with the evaporation. The acidity carries over as well. But keep in mind, the precipitate usually does not carry over flavours! Though some aromatics (like chocolate) do have some taste, like a mild bitterness, usually no flavours. Distilled apple juice will smell like apple juice but have no taste. And also, since the precipitate only has the aromatic component, the smell seems more intense since there are no other components mixing with it. The concentrate is simply that, a concentrate of the original liquid; this is similar to a reduction that's been boiling for a period of time.

Certain aromatics that were masked in the original liquid now become apparent in the precipitate. Perhaps those aromatics need to be balanced with the other components in the original liquid to taste good.

The fun here is that you can make something that looks like water but smell like something completely different.

Some interesting things to make: edible tobacco vanilla perfume, 'grappa' from crappy white wine, clear chocolate milk (inspired from Alinea).

Glassware

Cocktails can be served in various glasses. Whatever can hold a liquid is considered a container and I consider that container part of the glassware family. Here you are some common glasses category:

- Shot
- Snifter
- Stemware glass: Martini, Nick and Nora, coupe
- Old fashioned glass/short tumbler
- Tankard
- Julep
- Highball/Long drinks
- Wine glass
- Champagne flûte

Very important: remember to always use chilled glasses in order to prevent changes in temperature that will negatively affect the drink. Better if you can keep them in a freezer.

Also, special attention must be dedicated to the glass volume.
This is essential in order to know if the drink will fit perfectly inside the glass and here are some tips to consider when creating a drink:

1. find out the volume of the glass.
2. measure the amount of the drink by adding the quantity of the ingredients used.

3. forecast the quantity that will be created in the shaking/ stirring, throwing process also known as dilution.
4. measure the ice's volume (the formula is: side times side times side).
5. by adding the amount of the drink + dilution + ice's volume, you will now know if the drink fit inside the glass and have the perfect wash line.

Did you know...
The wash line is the point where the surface or the top of the drink touches the glass.

Techniques

Shake

It is a very simple method and one of the most common ways to mix a drink.

Combine the ingredients into a shaker tin, add the ice, and then the magic happens. This is useful when the liquids have different densities. As a general rule, almost all drinks that have sugar and/or citrus juice are shaken as this is the best way to mix these ingredients together. Shake around 10 seconds to have a -5°C temperature, so for a short time. Shaken drinks are also aerated. Use when the egg is present. Remember always to strain or double strain the drinks after shaking to avoids any eventually pieces of fruit or especially ice to drop into the drink although sometimes the small pieces of ice, called diamonds can have a great effect on your drink.

The dry shake – you should always dry shake a cocktail with egg white without ice in order to emulsify the egg and then with the ice to create the foam. You can do also the reverse dry shake which I prefer more.

Squeeze some citrus essential oils on top of foam to remove the smell of the egg.

The positive aspect using egg white in the drink is that you will have a creamy texture but keep in mind that the foam will block the flavours of the drink and in addition using the egg white is not vegan friendly (you can use an alternative such as chickpea water, soapbark).

Japanese shake. The inventor of this *hard shake* technique – an extremely gentle and theatrical way of shaking a drink in a tree piece shaker, is Kazuo Uyeda, a very famous Japanese bartender, the owner of Tender Bar. He swings the shaker gently from side to side. This is done to swirl the liquids inside the shaker for maximum aeration and at the same time reduce the speed of the ice hitting the bottom or top of the shaker.

Did you know...
When shaking you will incorporate tiny air bubbles. These bubbles contain aromatic flavour molecules of the ingredients used that will be released on the palate when drinking. For this reason is very important to serve the shaken drinks fast.

Stir is another popular way of mixing method. It is used for drinks with a similar consistency. Stir at least 40 seconds to have a - 4°C temperature cocktail. Over stirring or under stirring can negatively affect the drink as for the temperature and dilution. It is suitable for mixing those cocktails which, containing particularly delicate ingredients such as distilled spirits, wines, and liqueurs (defined in jargon 'clear'), that must be simply mixed and not shaken with the shaker.

Build. Some drinks are built directly in the glass, for example a Negroni, but is very important to mix the ingredients inside the glass with a bar spoon up-down as they have different densities so the heavier will go down and the lightest will stay on top; try to avoid this. It is made in the glass in which the cocktail is served and usually a swizzle stick is put into the glass, allowing the drinker to mix them more if desired.

Blending. Use an electric blender when the recipes contain fruit or any other ingredients which don't break down by shaking. The result is a smooth ready to serve mixture and I highly recommend to use for egg white style cocktails such as Whiskey Sour, Pisco Sour, White Lady.

Layering. To layer or float an ingredient use the back of the spoon in order to have success. Use this technique for an Irish coffee and a White Russian.

Flaming is the method by which a cocktail is set alight, normally to enhance the flavour of a drink. One of the most famous flaming drinks is the Blue Blazer.

Rolling. When you roll a drink, you're simply pouring the contents of one glass into another glass. Do this a few times and you have a perfectly mixed drink.

Rolling can be used instead of shaking or stirring with the aim to mix without adding too much dilution and to slightly aerate the drink.

Drinks like Bloody Mary and other cocktails 'on the rocks' benefit the most from rolling.

How to Roll a Drink

Before you begin rolling cocktails and risk wasting precious liquor, practice this technique with water and ice. To avoid cleaning up the floor, you might also want to begin outside until you get confident.

Fill one glass with ice and add the liquid ingredients.

Pour the contents from this glass into a shaker tin or mixing glass, holding the ice with a strainer.

Pour the contents back into the original glass.

Continue these last two steps up to five times then strain or pour everything into the serving glass.

Throwing. This technique is similar to the rolling and often exchanged for that in error, but the difference stands in the fact that the liquid is thrown together with the ice from one recipient to another. Repeat this process several times. Use when having very thick liquid ingredients (a Bloody Mary for example).

Swizzling is originally a food preparation technique that requires a utensil called swizzle stick that needs to be spun between the palms, lifted and submerged in a mixture.

From a liquid perspective, a non-alcoholic precursor to swizzle drinks was *Switchel*, a spiced mix of water and vinegar that was sweetened with honey or molasses.

Infusion is the process of extracting chemical compounds or flavours in a solvent such as water, oil or alcohol, by allowing the material to remain suspended in the solvent over time (a process often called steeping). An infusion is also the name for the resultant liquid. The process of infusion is distinct from decoction, which involves boiling, or percolation, in which the liquid passes through the material (as in a coffeemaker). To make the infusion you have to consider the size of the particles to be infused, their weight, the temperature, pressure used, time and alcohol content. Smaller is the particles, faster will infuse. Some ingredients extract better in a shorter time, and sometimes a long extraction, especially with herbs can result in bitter components. A warm infusion will be faster than a cold infusion.

Try infusing some bergamot leaves in vodka overnight using freezing temperature. Using very low temperature you will extract just the aromatic flavours without extracting the colour and the bitter components.

Maceration is the most common form of infusion. Try to steep into a bottle of vodka some berries and you will have a flavoured vodka. Add sugar and you will have a liqueur.

Pressure infusion. There are several techniques to infuse a liquid with another ingredient and all of them simply consists of placing the solid ingredient in the liquid and leaving it there until the aroma of the ingredient gets absorbed by the liquid. This technique is done under pressure, in a vacuum or at low temperatures. The amount of time required to infuse the liquid depends on type of liquid and the solid ingredient used.

Rapid infusion with the iSi Whip, created by Dave Arnold, Director of Culinary Technology of The French Culinary Institute. Very easy to do it: put the solid flavourful ingredient in the iSi Whip, fill with the liquid to be infused, charge it with N2O, swirl, wait for a minute or so, vent the gas out of the whipper and strain the infused liquid.

Pressure infusion works by creating a highly pressured environment inside the container where the ingredients are surrounded by the liquid. The combination of high pressure plus agitation and right amount of time allows the ingredients' flavours and essences to be squeezed directly into the beverage fluid.

You can infuse flavours into alcohol, oils, water, cream using flavourful ingredients like herbs, spices, seeds, fruits and others.

Cold ingredients will result in a weaker infusion. Use warm or room temperature foods and liquids for the most flavourful results.

Carbonation

One of my favourite ingredients, carbonation is the process that is associated with bubbles and is defined as the saturation of a liquid with CO_2 gas.

The formula to have a great carbonated drink includes temperature + pressure + surface contact.

- The liquid is able to absorb more CO_2 when it is cold and ideally is to have a temperature close to the freezing point.
- Pressure is what forces the liquid to absorb the CO_2. The amount of CO_2 present inside the drink dictates the effervescence on the palate as well as the aroma when the bubble opens in the mouth plus the flavour brought to the nose and keep in mind also the fact that CO_2 brings the alcohol in blood faster so can get drunk faster.

- Surface contact between CO_2 and the fluid is where the absorption happens, so try to increase the contact surface so you can inject more bubbles into your drink. Keep in mind that a very important characteristic of the carbonation is not the dimension of the bubbles but the amount of CO_2 present in the drink.

When carbonating a drink avoid protein ingredients as will foam and also avoid overcharging the recipients for pressure, especially when using soda stream for more than a third. Better carbonating a low abv drink with clarified ingredients in order to have excellent results. Be careful not to increase the pressure too much otherwise it could cause serious damage to both you and your equipment.

Aging. This is an old practice to store everything, even dead bodies (Admiral Nelson's body was stored in rum to the way back home after died in the battle of Trafalgar). In the case of the barrel aging consider that can be used a cask made of different types of wood, charred or not, refilled or not, previously contained sherry, bourbon or vinegar, therefore can impart the previous characteristics to your aging liquid. The size of the barrel and the time aged are very important factors; smaller means more contact with wood so more complex, and too much contact means too many flavours. As an alternative, it can be used a wood infusion into the liquid. Some winemakers used to infuse wood staves to impart woody flavours to their wine.

Dehydrating is a fun, cost-effective, and easy way to prepare foods and fruits for garnishing your cocktail, for storage, or even for snacking right away. It is very simple and incredibly healthy as dehydrated foods retain their vitamin and mineral content.

A food dehydrator is a small kitchen appliance that is used to dry or dehydrate your food. Utilizing a built-in fan and low amounts of heat, this small appliance uses a light flow of hot air to reduce the overall amount of water found in fruits, veggies, meats and other foods. Once the water is removed, the food won't spoil as quickly as it normally would, and it is also impervious to many kinds of bacteria that would otherwise grow. A food dehydrator allows you to retain all of those nutrients and vitamins within your fruits and especially can be used to avoid any fruit waste. The temperature and time required to adequately dehydrate will vary depending on the type of dehydrator you buy, as well as the fruit you want to dehydrate. General time and temperature guidelines will be printed on the dehydrator label or included in the instruction manual along with suggested times needed. In order to be stored properly, foods need to be at least 95% dehydrated.

Smoking is one of the oldest food preservation methods, probably having arisen shortly after the development of cooking with fire. The practice attained high levels of sophistication in several cultures, notably the smoking of fish in Scandinavia and north-western North America and the production of smoked hams in Europe and the United States. Interest in smoking meats declined during the mid-20th century owing to the popularity of chemical preservatives.

In modern days, the smoking process is better understood and has the role not just in preserving but also to flavour (increasing the food palatability), browning (imparting a rich brown colour), cooking.

It is done by exposing the food to smoke from burning or smouldering material, most often wood. Most of the positive aromatic effects of smoke derived from the breaking down of the lignin present in the wood.

Use the smoking gun to easily direct the smoke into the desired vessel, cloche, mixing beaker, or glass. The draw of air through the crucible causes the smouldering wood to heat sufficiently without catching alight.

The type of wood used will have a bearing on the type of smoke that is produced. Some examples: hickory (sweet aromatic aroma, is used typically on a barbeque); apple (lighter aromatic, but a pleasant fruity characteristic); oak (very bold and intense, use carefully to do overpower); mesquite (strong and rich aromatics).

Clarification. The roots of this technique are very deep in the past and according to cocktail historian Dave Wondrich, using milk to clarify a punch has been practiced since at least the early 18th century. Since many punches are acidic, milk was added in an attempt to mitigate its effects on the stomach. This is still a very common technique in modern days and can be used different types of milk such as cow, sheep, or even vegetable milk: almond, oat, soya, etc.

This technique consists in removing suspended particles and separating clear liquids from cloudy solids. The reasons to clarify a liquid can be countless –purer looking drink, great potential for a good carbonation outcome, incorporating a silky texture.

There are several clarification techniques and before you decide which technique to use you need to evaluate your liquid – how long it's going to last, if its heat-stable, its acidity, and the density of the liquid.

Filter clarification – blocks particles allowing only the clear ones to come through. This type of clarification requires very fine strainers.

Gel clarification – particles are trapped in a gel and then the clear liquid leaks out. Firstly, you need to incorporate your gelling agent into the liquid and then decide whether to use a freezing process or agar.

When agar is used, keep in mind that needs to be heated to a boil to be dispersed into the liquid.

Many advantages: vegetarian-friendly, leaks more than gelatine, the gel is formed before the process begins so you can verify that it will work, much faster process. The negative aspect is that it needs to be boiled to fully incorporate. This method doesn't work for liquids that don't last long such as citrus juice.

Centrifuge clarification – much quicker and effective although the most expensive option, centrifuge spins the liquid using a high speed and gravitational pull.

Egg white –traditionally used to filter impurities from liquids.

A **rotavap** is commonly used and also the most expensive option.

Did you know...
Hydrocolloids are a family of compounds that can be used to thicken liquids, strengthen ice creams, create alcoholic jellies and jams, stabilize foams and airs, emulsify fats into an aqueous (water-based) solution and create fluid gels. Use xanthan gum into your sugar syrup and you will have an elastic, firmer texture.

Gelification is defined as the process of turning a substance into a gelatinous form. With this process, liquid substances are converted into solids with the help of a gelling agent. Common gelling agents come from natural sources and include agar-agar, gelatine, carrageenan, gellan gum, pectin, and methylcellulose. More often these gelling agents are presented in a dry, solid form that needs to be hydrated.

It can serve to stabilize liquids without affecting taste. It may also be used for suspending food particles and creating various shapes for aesthetic purposes. Lastly, it can also be used to create various textures and improve dining experiences.

Most of them result in some kind of solid structure that traps liquid in it. The structure is often made of proteins and gives form and body to the gel.

There are many different gelling ingredients. Below is a short description of several gelling agents:

Agar-agar (usually abbreviated as agar) creates brittle gels, and it must be brought to a boil to hydrate. It sets at room temperature and can be heated to 80°C (176°F) before melting.

Agar is typically used in a ratio of 0.2% to 3.0%. For soft gels a 0.2% to 0.5% range is ideal, and the gel becomes harder as more agar is added. Locust bean gum can be added to make the gel more elastic, usually by replacing 10% of the agar with locust bean gum.

Gelatine needs to be dispersed in hot liquid to form elastic gel.

The ratio indicated range from 0.5% to 1.0% for soft, tender gels. For very hard, firm gels can be used in ratios of upwards 6% but the typical range for medium-firm gels is 1% to 3%.

If you are using sheet gelatine you will use 0.3 to 0.5 sheets per 100 grams of liquid for soft gels and 0.5 to 1.66 sheets per 100 grams of liquid for firmer gels. For very firm gels more than 3.3 sheets per 100 grams of liquid are sometimes used.

Methylcellulose has the uncommon ability to gel as it heats and melt as it cools. There are many different types of methylcellulose available for a variety of uses. For making foams, a ratio mixture of 1.0 to 2.0% Methocel F50 with 0.1 to 0.3% xanthan gum is commonly used. For gels, a ratio range of 0.25 to 3.0% Methocel A4C is a good starting point.

Lecithin is ideal for making not just foams but also airs mousses and emulsions. Most commercial lecithin is extracted from soybeans, making it both vegetarian and vegan friendly. Lecithin contains both hydrophobic (water-hating) and hydrophilic (water-loving) groups, so it can also be used in making emulsions. Under normal circumstances oil and water do not mix and separate out, creating two distinct layers, but an emulsifier such as lecithin helps to combine these two layers, creating a more stable preparation.

Soya lecithin should be used in a concentration of 0.3to 0.8% for foam and 0.5 to 1% for emulsions.

Foaming this is another way to make your drink more interesting. It is different than air (light foam) through its creaminess, rich mouthfeel, and viscosity. It is not complex if you think of a pint of Guinness or a cappuccino. Using fresh egg white in drinks is the most common option used. Pasteurised and powdered egg white (albumin) are other options even though are not vegan friendly and contain allergies.

Other alternatives are represented by some egg-free hydrocolloids that we just covered earlier and use in 1% ratio powder to liquid normally.

For the foam to hold its shape for a period of time there must be some form of thickening or gelling agent present in the liquid and adding a touch of xanthan gum (a popular food additive that's commonly added to foods as a thickener or stabilizer) your foam will highly benefit.

Once you have mixed the ingredients place them in a cream whipper and then 'charge it' using nitrous dioxide ($N2O$) to be whipped.

Fermentation is a mechanism that consists of converting carbohydrates to alcohol or organic acids using microorganisms – yeasts or bacteria – under anaerobic conditions and there are two types of fermentation: lactic acid fermentation – when yeasts and bacteria convert starches or sugars into lactic acid in foods like pickles, sauerkraut, sourdough bread, and yogurt, and alcoholic fermentation that produces alcohol and carbon dioxide.

Pickling. In short, pickling is a process that consists of preserving or extending the shelf life of food by either anaerobic fermentation in brine or immersion in vinegar.

This wonderful operation is mainly utilized for solid ingredients, changing their taste, flavour, and texture, however, can be used to substitute the citrus' acidity in cocktails by pickling juices and one of my favourite is pickled mango juice to use in a spicy Margarita.

Fat washing. An old perfumer's technique called enfleurage, the fat washing is another great technique that will incorporate creaminess into your cocktail and consist in infusing rich fat-based savoury ingredients such as oils, butter, avocados, bacon, etc into alcohol and using lower temperatures, the liquid is then frozen and the fat is separated due to the different freezing points. You still need to first transform your chosen fat into a liquid form and combine it with the alcohol and then filtered it various times through coffee filters or cheesecloth for optimal results.

This technique is possible as alcohol can dissolve oil-based molecules and the ratio suggested is 6 parts alcohol to 1 part fat for powerful tasting fats and 3 to 1 for less powerful fats such as oils and butter.

Grilling is another personal favourite technique and consists of using direct or indirect heat applied to the surface of the food ingredients. The great aspect of this technique is that will caramelize the sugars present in the ingredient used for the cocktail and will give wonderful flavour notes, depth and complexity to the final result.

Spherification. The process is linked with the renowned chef Ferran Adrià. Spherification is a magic process that creates a gel around a liquid, forming a gelled sphere with a liquid centre. Sodium alginate (a thickening agent extracted from seaweed) is commonly used in spherification because of its ability to gel in the presence of calcium ions such as calcium chloride, lactate or gluconate lactate.

Calcium gluconate lactate for its neutral flavour is the most suitable for reverse and frozen reverse spherification (my favourite as can be prepared in advance and last up to three days when conserved in water or preferably in the liquid that has been used to make the drink – ex: Negroni sphere in Negroni liquid).

The difference between reverse spherification and direct spherification is where the gelling agent is put: in reverse spherification, the gelling agents are added to the setting bath, while in direct spherification is placed in the base.

It can be dispersed and hydrated at almost any temperature and the gels are very heat tolerant. For direct spherification, a 0.5% to 1% sodium alginate base is used with a 0.5% to 1% calcium gluconate lactate setting bath. For reverse spherification a 1.0% to 3.0% calcium gluconate lactate base is used with a 0.4% to 0.5% sodium alginate bath.

Ice

Ice is water frozen into a solid-state and is the most important, and most neglected, component of the cocktail making.

A bit of history

Ice has long been valued as a means of cooling and in 400 BC in Iran, Persian engineers had already mastered the technique of storing ice in the middle of summer in the desert. The ice was brought in during the winters from nearby mountains in bulk amounts, and stored in specially designed, naturally cooled refrigerators, called yakhchāl (meaning ice storage), and was used to chill treats for royalty.

There were thriving industries in 16th and 17th century in England, where low-lying areas along the Thames Estuary were flooded during the winter, and ice harvested in carts and stored inter-seasonally in insulated wooden houses, often located in large country houses. It was widely used to keep fish fresh when caught in distant waters. Ice was imported into England from Norway on a considerable scale as early as 1823.

In the United States, the first cargo of ice was sent from New York City to Charleston, South Carolina in 1799, and by the first half of the 19th century, ice harvesting had become a profitable business.

The concept of quality ice started in 1805. Frederic Tudor, the man who was dubbed the Ice King, shipped ice from the lakes of Massachusetts all over the globe. It was considered a luxury to have your drink served with 'Tudor's Ice'. The advent of artificial refrigeration technology has since made the delivery of ice obsolete.

Why we use ice in a cocktail

Chefs use fire to cook their ingredients and bartenders use ice to 'cook' theirs. It is often described as a universal ingredient for almost every cocktail made (with the obvious exception of hot drinks).

It is used when serving a drink on ice and also when preparing the drink with the shaking, stirring, swizzling, or rolling technique and its role is not only to chill drinks but to add dilution and make the drink more palatable by lowering the ABV of the final result although the alcohol content will be the same.

Consider that diluted ice from shaking and stirring can be between 10%-25% of your final cocktail.

A low temperature drink means that will be refreshing and clean on the palate, but the colder a drink is, the less flavour it has.

It is important to use clear ice, as it indicates purity. Cloudy ice forms because of impurities in the water and because oxygen bubbles get trapped. Oxygen in your ice will make it melt quicker and impurities can impart flavour into your drink.

It is also essential to use the right ice for the right drink and to use always fresh ice (cold and not melted) to preserve your drinks for longer without ruining them.

Homemade clear ice

If you decide to make homemade ice, keep in mind that the tap water might contain chlorine and other chemicals that can negatively contribute to your ice, but also most of the freezers freeze from outside to inside and this means that all the impurities and oxygen rather than being expelled, will be trapped inside your 'ice'.

Furthermore, avoid storing the ice in the freezer near foods like fish or anything else – you don't want your Old Fashioned to taste of mackerel.

To make perfect homemade clear ice start with the water: distilled water seems to be perfect. (Distilled water is water that has had many of its impurities removed by distillation.

Distillation involves boiling the water and then condensing the steam into a clean container). Bottled water may or may not be distilled, so be sure to check the label. Next, it's also crucial to get rid of as much air as you can. Tiny air bubbles that become trapped in the ice as the water freezes, will make your ice cloudy, and it's this imperfection that causes cloudy ice to melt faster than clear ice. To allow most of the air to escape, boil your water, even if is distilled water.

Let the water cool after the boil and cover it with a lid or clean aluminium foil to prevent any dust or other bits of dirt from spoiling your project.

At this point fill the cooler no more than halfway with your prepared water and place it in the freezer with the lid off. This allows the top surface of the water to come in contact with the cold air of your freezer, while the bottom portion remains insulated in the cooler. As the ice freezes, the impurities will be pushed to the bottom of the cooler.

The trick is to remove the cooler from the freezer before the ice has frozen completely so that you can harvest the clear ice block and pour away the impurities with the remaining unfrozen water. Allow the cooler to sit at room temperature for a half-hour or so, or until you can lessen the block of ice. Use an ice pick to chip off bits of ice for drinks or use a serrated knife to score the block into large cubes before using a mallet and chisel or your ice pick to break it up.

If you prefer regular ice cubes or ice balls, fill ice moulds with prepared water and place them in the cooler. Then surround your moulds with more water to keep them insulated and allow the same top-down freezing method to work as noted above.

Ice types

There is a type of ice for each type of drink: cubes for shaking, spheres or larger cubes for rocks drinks, and for highballs, pebbles, or crushed ice for tiki-style drinks.

Cube ice

Very little in the cocktail making is simpler than this. Ice cubes are good for almost all mixing: for shaking, stirring, drinks on the rocks, or with juices and sodas. The larger, thicker surface area is, the slower and less dilution will be the result.

With the help of a Lewis bag, a similar canvas sack, or a clean towel, cubes can also be pounded into cracked or crushed pieces. The only other thing you need for this is a blunt object (i.e. hammer, mallet, muddler) and some unwanted frustration that needs to get out. It's a little bit of work but quite therapeutic.

Crushed ice

Crushed or shaved as often is called (similar but to be more precise, crushed ice is when you break the ice in pieces while shaved ice is when you rub ice with something sharp so it becomes thin) is famous primarily used for frozen drinks and juleps. You can make crushed ice in a couple of different ways. Easiest, perhaps, is to use a blender after obviously the use of a crushed ice machine. A fair portion of the ice will melt, though, just from the heat of the motor, so you might want to drain off excess liquid, so you don't water down your cocktails.

Cracked ice

Smaller than cubes, cracked ice melts faster and adds more water to drinks. Usually, this is used when making frozen drinks because cubes can block the blender's blade. Two-thirds to one cup of cracked ice is perfect for a single frozen Daiquiri or Margarita.

Ice block

Back in the days, all of the bartenders used ice block and it was up to the individual and their ice tools and skills to create smaller, usable chunks and shavings for mixing. Nowadays there is a rebirth of reusing ice blocks.

Ice ball

Another large chunk of ice that is becoming more popular is the ice ball, which is commonly used for serving 'cocktails on the rocks'.

Something cool to do is to flavour the ice cubes by dipping the ice into warm oils aromatized with different spices, herbs, fruit, etc.

Did you know...

Dry ice

Dry Ice is the common name for solid carbon dioxide (CO_2). It gets this name because it does not melt into a liquid when heated; instead, it changes directly into a gas (this process is known as sublimation.)

When carbon dioxide reaches a solid-state, we call it 'dry ice', and this material is used in all sorts of applications. Carbon dioxide is found naturally within the earth's atmosphere, and it's the gas that we humans exhale and plants use during the process of photosynthesis. Carbon dioxide is denser than air and is transformed into a solid when placed under pressure at a low temperature of -109°F/-42°C.

What can be used for?

Fog effect – Dry ice when combined with hot water will produce an awe-inspiring display of bubbling water and thick voluminous fog. Use a pound of dry ice for every 4L of hot water for 5–10 minutes of maximum effect.

Since dry ice retains a temperature of -78°C, the water will cool rapidly. Replace with hot water to maintain the desired effect. Avoid place inside the drink (to avoid being swallow).

Freezing fruit – Carbon dioxide bubbles become trapped in the fruit, making it fizzy and carbonated. Place dry ice in the bottom of your cooler and the fruit directly on top. Close cooler and let fruits freeze for 20–30 minutes. Remove fruit and place in freezer-safe plastic bags as needed.

Dry ice ice cream – You can use dry ice to make instant ice cream. Because carbon dioxide gas is released, the resulting ice cream is bubbly and carbonated, sort of like an ice cream float.

Carbonate liquids– When dry ice is added to liquids, the dry ice will sublime and become a gaseous CO2 vapor. During this process, the liquid will absorb the CO2 gas and become a carbonated liquid.

Is it safe?

Dry ice itself is not poisonous, but the surface of the solid is very cold and if you ever have a chance to handle dry ice, you want to be sure to wear heavy gloves. The super-cold surface temperature can easily damage your skin if you touch it directly. For the same reason, you never want to taste or swallow dry ice, either.

Another important concern with dry ice is ventilation. You want to make sure the area where stored is well-ventilated. Carbon dioxide is heavier than air, and it can concentrate in low areas or enclosed spaces (like a car or a room where dry ice is sublimating). Normal air is 78% nitrogen, 21% oxygen, and only 0.035% carbon dioxide. If the concentration of carbon dioxide in the air rises above 5%, carbon dioxide can become toxic. Be sure to ventilate any area that contains dry ice, and do not transport it in a closed vehicle.

Did you know...

Liquid nitrogen

Sometimes liquid nitrogen is denoted LN2, LN, or LIN. It is nitrogen that is cold enough to exist in liquid form. It consists of two nitrogen atoms sharing covalent bonds (N2) and was first liquefied on April 15, 1883, by Polish physicists Zygmunt Wróblewski and Karol Olszewski.

At normal atmospheric temperatures and pressure, nitrogen exists as gas all around us in the atmosphere. To turn it into a liquid, it needs to be cooled to a temperature between -346º F and -320.44º F (-210º C and -195.8º C).

Liquid nitrogen looks a lot like boiling water. It can be kept up to a few weeks in a special pressurized and vented container called a Dewar. Since it boils at a temperature of -320.4º F (-195.7º C), liquid nitrogen turns into nitrogen vapor very quickly when released into the atmosphere at room temperature.

When this happens, you will see a lot of fog, which is made up of condensed water vapor that has been cooled by exposure to liquid nitrogen.

What is used for?

Liquid nitrogen has many uses, mainly based on its cold temperature and low reactivity. Examples of common applications include: freezing and transport of food products; cryopreservation of biological samples, such as sperm, eggs, and animal genetic samples; cryotherapy to remove skin abnormalities; in cryosurgery, a super-chilled scalpel may be used to remove cancer tissue; for quick freezing of water or pipes to allow work on them when valves aren't available; cooling materials for easier machining or fracturing.

What interests us is its use for the molecular gastronomy preparation of foods and beverages, so this means that is possible to prepare ice cream; freezing fruits and then watching them shatter when tapped onto a hard surface and to create dense fog effects for a variety of situations, such as in movies and haunted houses.

Liquid Nitrogen Safety

Liquid nitrogen is very useful, but it's not always easy to work with. Fortunately, it's not flammable, nontoxic, and doesn't react readily with other chemicals. It's also odourless, colourless. However, it's extremely cold and can cause extreme frostbite in living tissue.

When working with liquid nitrogen, it's important to do so in a large, well-ventilated area. As it boils, one litre of liquid nitrogen expands to nearly 700 litres of nitrogen vapor. This expansion creates a lot of pressure and could cause an explosion in a sealed container, for example. It also displaces oxygen in the immediate area, creating a danger of asphyxiation in an area without sufficient ventilation. Cold nitrogen gas is heavier than air, so the risk is greatest near the ground.

Liquid nitrogen is stored in special insulated containers that are vented to prevent pressure build-up. Depending on the design of the flask, it can be stored for hours up to a few weeks.

Cocktail

The etymology of the term *cocktail* is not clear, however, there are several hypotheses about its origin: it could derive from the English terms *cock* (rooster) and *tail* (tail), perhaps because around 1400 in the English countryside a colourful drink was drank inspired by the colours of the *cock's tail*. Alternatively, it could derive from the French term coquetier, an egg container that was used in New Orleans to serve liquor during the nineteenth century.

The first written appearance is believed to come from the US: May 13th, 1806 a newspaper of Hudson, *The Balance and Columbian Repository* mentioned the word, but on March 16th, 1798, in London, UK, a newspaper *The Morning Post and Gazetteer*, reported that a pub owner won a lottery and erased all his customers' debits.

The week after, the newspaper, satirically reported that one of the debts was a *cocktail.*

The first publication of a guide that included cocktail recipes was written in 1862: *How to Mix Drinks or The Bon Vivant's Companion*, by Professor Jerry Thomas. In addition to the list of the usual drinks with liquor mix, there were written 10 recipes that were called 'Cocktails'.

The ingredient that differentiated the 'cocktails' from other drinks in this compendium was the use of bitters, even if this type of ingredient is now almost no longer found in modern recipes.

In the early 1800s a *cocktail* was a mixed drink containing liquor, sugar, and bitters, and anything else had a different name. 'Cocktails' retained their original definition until sometime in the late 1800s, when more ingredients became available and were incorporated into the old recipes. In the early 1900s, the definition was further expanded to include nearly all mixed drinks concocted in a shaker – which was most of them.

Nowadays, 'cocktail' is a catch-all term for 'mixed drinks', no matter the ingredient or the preparation.

A cocktail is a drink obtained through a proportionate and balanced mixture of different alcoholic, non-alcoholic, and flavouring ingredients. A well-executed cocktail must have a balanced structure, aroma, and colour.

Ingredients

The key to a great recipe is balance; each ingredient contributes to the level of sweetness, acidity, bitterness, alcohol, and aroma.

The ingredients can be subdivided into:

Base: is the element around which the cocktail is made; this is the primary source that gives structure to the drink (spirits, liqueurs, fortified wines, non-alcoholic base, etc).

Flavouring: The flavouring is the element that enriches the olfactory and gustative range: liqueurs, fortified wines, cordials, syrups, bitters are normally the most used ones that give aroma and taste.

Bitter: A bitter is an aromatic flavouring agent, made from infusing roots, barks, fruit peels, seeds, spices, herbs, flowers, and many other botanicals in high proof alcohol or sometimes glycerine with a low sugar content. Long reputed to possess medicinal properties, bitters were billed for the cure to whatever ailed you, nowadays it is essential and commonly used in the cocktail industry.

Sweetness: it is crucial the sweetness in a drink; it must be the best one and unique. This can be present not just inside the drink but also as a rim garnish so will affect in a sweet way your perception of the drink. It can be used not just in syrups but also preserves, agave, honey, maple syrup, treacle, molasses, etc. Can be made from one ingredient or multiple.

Did you know...

A liqueur is an alcoholic beverage made from a distilled spirit that has been flavoured with fruit, cream, herbs, spices, flowers or nuts and bottled with added sugar or other sweeteners. Liqueurs are typically quite sweet; they are usually not aged for long after the ingredients are mixed but may have resting periods during their production to allow flavours to mingle.

Sourness is associated with **acidity**. Lemon and lime juice are the most common sour fruits that we can found at the bar and use for their acidity.

Here is a list of the most common acids that can be used singularly or that can be combined to obtain surprising flavours:

Citric acid is an organic acid found most abundantly in fruits (especially citrus fruits) like lemons, limes, grapefruit, and oranges; it has a refreshing clean taste. Consider that the acidity of freshly squeezed citrus juices change very shortly after has been extracted. It doesn't necessarily means that change negatively. Ideally is to use fresh juice in the process of creating the drink.

Ascorbic acid is found naturally in citrus fruits and many vegetables. Ascorbic acid is an essential nutrient in human diets, and necessary to maintain connective tissue and bone. Its biologically active form, vitamin C, functions as a reducing agent and coenzyme in several metabolic pathways. Alone does not have a lot of flavours and doesn't give much acidity. Used as an antioxidant – prevents the juices from oxidizing.

Acetic acid, also known as ethanoic acid and methane carboxylic acid, is a colourless liquid that has a strong and distinct pungent and sour smell; it is most well-known because of its presence in vinegar. It is the only alimentary acid common that can be aromatized.

Lactic acid. Among the bacteria responsible for lactic fermentation is the lactic acid bacteria.

Lactic fermentation is a bacterial process that takes place during the production of numerous food products. It provides the final products with characteristic aromas and textures and plays a crucial role in food safety and hygiene.

In winemaking, lactic acid bacteria are doubly important as they can both enhance and diminish the quality of the wine. They are responsible for malolactic fermentation, but they can also cause changes that adversely affect the organoleptic properties of the final product. It has the pickles taste and cheeses.

Malic acid is a component of many of the foods that we eat daily. The food that is most well known for its high malic acid content is the apple. Other fruits with a very high concentration of the acid are nectarines, cherries, lychees, bananas, mangoes, peaches, tomatoes, and strawberries; it is also used as a flavour enhancer for many drinks and candies. It is especially common in diet sodas and other artificially sweetened drinks. Has the flavours of a caramelized apple. It has a longer taste compared to citric acid.

Tartaric acid. The most important organic acids in grapes are tartaric and malic acids, comprising about 70% to 90% of the total grape's acidity. The precursors of the organic acids are produced in the vine leaves and after they are synthesized into acids in grape berries. At ripening, the acidity level of grapes is an important parameter to determine the quality of wines. Has the flavour of caramelized rugged grape.

Phosphoric acid is the only inorganic acid in this list.

It's a common additive in many processed foods. Manufacturers use it to add flavour and maintain freshness.

Phosphoric acid is a colourless, odourless crystalline liquid and gives the soft drinks a tangy flavour and prevents the growth of mould and bacteria, which can multiply easily in a sugary solution. Most of the soda's acidity also comes from phosphoric acid.

Phosphoric acid is made from the mineral phosphorus, which is also found naturally in the body. It works with calcium to form strong bones and teeth. It also helps support kidney function and the way your body uses and stores energy. Phosphorus helps your muscles recover after a hard workout. The mineral plays a major role in the body's growth and is even needed to produce DNA and RNA, the genetic codes of living things.

Phosphorus is synthetically produced by first being turned into phosphorus pentoxide through a chemical manufacturing process. It's then treated again to become phosphoric acid.

It is very dry and strong.

Dilution

Dilution is also very important because will lower down the abv of the drink to a more palatable level and provide space for the flavour to interact. Obviously, too much water and the drink will be flat.

The following are some factors that will influence the dilution: the quality, the size and temperature of the ice, temperature and consistency of ingredients, the mixing vessel and its temperature, the technique used and its timeframe.

For example, to make a Dry Martini, using a room temperature gin and vermouth (around 22°C), stirring for around 40 seconds in a cold metal mixing glass over regular ice cubes you will end with a drink at -4°C approximately and adding around 15 ml dilution water from the melting process of the ice.

The Garnish

The first sip of any drink is with the eye. A nice-looking cocktail will taste better and ideally the garnishes should be done before preparing the drink.

The garnish serves to improve the aesthetic impact of the drink; sometimes it can also vary the aroma of the cocktail, such as the 'crustas', that is sugar or salt passed on the edge of the dampened glass. Usually, we use fruit (peelings or cloves of citrus, cherries in spirit, olives) or flavourings (sugar, salt, cocoa, nutmeg).

The garnish has to evolve with the drink but remember that are drinks that no need the garnish because of their spectacular aroma and because they are already attractive looking.

Did you know...

When squeezing essential oils from a citrus peel make sure you use a 90 degrees angle and a distance of approx. 4.5cm.

The reason is because in the citrus peel, there are two types of oils:

- the *good* ones (very aromatic, light, and delicate) so they are very volatile.
- the *bad* ones (very bitter, so they affect negatively the drink; they are very heavy so if used correctly this simple technique we will avoid using them, therefore, avoid to influence negatively the drink).

Unit of measure

The dosage of ingredients in recipes can be indicated with different units of measure, according to necessity, technique, and nation. The main units of measurement are:

- Centilitres (cl) and millilitres (ml.): This is the most accurate unit of measure, as it allows very small dosages.

- Ounces (oz.): It is the most quantized and rapid unit of measurement, but less precise (one ounce equals 29 ml approx).

Then there are other units of measurement used:
1 bar spoon – 5 ml
1 dash- 0.8 ml
1 drop- 0.05 ml

Categories of drinks

The categorization according to the moment of consumption is mainly distinguished based on the effect given to the organism, dividing the compounds so the moment of consumption is distinguished on the basis of the dinner:

Pre-dinner: they are served as aperitifs, from the Latin *aperire* (open); many are characterized by the property of stimulating salivation and, consequently, appetite. Except for exceptions, they are characterized by the prevalence of bittering aromas.

After dinner: can be digestive or replace and/or accompany a dessert. They are characterized by the presence of bitters, liqueurs, and/or creams, a complex olfactory and gustatory composition, often combined with a strong alcoholic component.

Any time (known as well as all-day drink): under this term are included many cocktails, with very varied flavours but united by often fresh and refreshing flavours or desserts. They consist of a very variable alcohol base, the use of water softeners, fruit or non-alcoholic juices, and are often richly decorated.

The Highball falls into the category of 'any time' as it presents a very abundant presence of non-alcoholic components. It is long, refreshing, and often fizzy.

The following represents the cocktail family:

Smash. It is a drink that consists of fresh herbs and fruits that are crushed. A smash can be a julep, but a julep is not always a smash.

Julep is a drink consisting of spirits, sugar and mint served over crushed ice.

Daisy is a classic style of cocktail that dates to the late 1800s. It is a family of drinks with a ratio 2:1:1 that is basically a base spirit, a sweet part but not syrups (normally curacao, maraschino, etc), and citrus juice. Cosmopolitan, Sidecar can be some examples of this category.

Sour (1850 circa) is a simple drink with a ratio 2:1:½ – base spirit, citrus juice and a sweetener (such as syrups). Keep in mind that we are using this ratio in this book and if the drinks tend to be on the sour side, it can be adjusted by increasing the syrup ratio or decreasing the acidity ratio. Also, consider that fresh citrus juice has a different acidity than one squeezed 2, 4 or 6 hours earlier; consider the citrus ripeness, provenience, and other factors that can influence its acidity.

Highball (1870 circa) indicates a family of cocktails, especially long drinks, with a refreshing effect, composed of an alcoholic base to which is added the so-called filler (soda or another carbonated beverage). They are usually served in a tall glass (called Highball) with ice.

Collins is a sour that is built over ice and finished with soda water.

Fizz is a Collins that is shaken, and the most famous is the Ramos Gin Fizz.

Punch (1600 circa) from Sanskrit meaning 'five', as the drink was originally made with five ingredients: alcohol, sugar, lemon, water, and tea or spices.

Sling (1750 circa) According to all the old-timey manuals, Slings are made from gin primarily, a lump of sugar, and a few gratings of nutmeg. The word 'sling' is derived from the German 'schlingen', to gulp or swallow hastily, the transatlantic sling may have originally been a 'short' drink or dram.

Cobbler (1850 circa) is an old form of mixed drink. Along with the use of wine, another peculiarity of this cocktail is the refinement and care of the garnish, based on fresh seasonal fruit, a real luxury at that time, and the use of crushed ice, another novelty, that the barman they worked hand-armed with chisels like cobblers, a custom that seems to be the origin of his name. An extra-luxury product, therefore, destined to the beautiful world, as evidenced by the fact that it was served with straw and silver spoon (to allow you to consume the fruit without touching it with your hands) incorporated into the glass. The most notorious cobbler is the Sherry Cobbler.

Toddy is a drink made typically with a spirit base, water, some type of sugar, and spices. In its simplest form today, a hot toddy is usually a mixture of whiskey, cinnamon, hot water, honey, and lemon. The word 'toddy' itself stretches back to the British colonial era and is taken from the Hindi word tārī, which was a drink made from the fermented sap of toddy palm, hence the name. It was originally served cold but then started to be served hot first in Scotland apparently as a cold cure and then spread worldwide.

Alcohol intake

Standard drink size and alcohol intake recommendations vary around the world. In the United Kingdom, the measure to quantify the actual alcoholic content within a given volume of an alcoholic beverage used is the unit of alcohol, and 1 unit of alcohol corresponds to 10 ml which in turn corresponds to 7.94 g (alcohol has a different weight: 0.7946 g). Normally it takes an average adult around an hour to process one unit of alcohol so that there's none left in their bloodstream.

As alcoholic drinks come in different sizes and strengths the units are used to define how strong a drink is. Consider also that everyone has a different response to alcohol intake and there are some factors that influence this such as weight, height, sex.

Another very important factor, the food, slows down the absorption of alcohol and allows a better metabolization with a minor elevation of blood alcohol.

To keep health risks from alcohol to a low level, the UK Chief Medical Officers' (CMO) advise it is safest not to drink more than 14 units a week and both the daily and weekly guidelines must be met for a person to remain low risk.

According to various studies, women develop alcohol use disorders at lower levels of consumption compared to men, as scientists discovered that women produce smaller quantities of an enzyme alcohol dehydrogenase (ADH), which is responsible for breaking down alcohol in the body, and for this reason is recommended that the guideline for women to be fewer than 14 units per week.

What does ABV mean?

Alcohol by volume (abbreviated as abv) represents a measure used to define how much alcohol is contained in a given volume of an alcoholic beverage and is expressed as a percentage.

For example, a bottle of wine that shows 12% abv, means that on 100ml there are 12ml of alcohol and a glass of wine served 175ml, contains 2 units, and the full bottle -750ml- contains 9 units.

Here are some examples of units present in common drinks:

A glass of champagne (125ml glass, 12% ABV) contains 1.5 units

A pint of beer (1 pint, 4% ABV) contains 2.3 units

A pint of cider (1 pint, 4.5% ABV) contains 2.6 units

A single shot of spirit (25ml, 40% ABV) contains 1 unit

How to calculate the alcohol content in a cocktail

1. We start by calculating the quantity of alcohol present in every ingredient:
   (quantity used x abv of ingredient): 100 = ml alcohol present in the drink
2. Then calculate the total quantity of alcohol in ml by adding the ml of alcohol present in the drink.
3. Afterwards is calculated the grams of alcohol multiplying the total ml for the specific weight of the alcohol
4. Lastly we calculate the abv of the cocktail using the following formula:
   (ml alcohol x 100) : (quantity cocktail + dilution) = abv cocktail

Keep in mind that water content is added by stirring this drink and is very important as changing the abv of the final drink. We are not treating the dilution subject this time but we will use 25% dilution for this calculation.

For example, let's take a Negroni with the following recipe:

30ml gin at 40% abv
30ml vermouth sweet at 16% abv
30ml bitter at 25% abv

1. 30 x 40: 100 = 12 ml alcohol
   30 x 16: 100 = 4.8 ml alcohol
   30 x 25: 100 = 7.5 ml alcohol

2. 12 + 4.8 + 7.5 = 24.3 ml of alcohol present in the cocktail

3. 24.9 x 0.79 = 19.671 g of alcohol present in the cocktail
4. (24.3 x 100): (90 + 22.5) = 21.6% abv of our Negroni

How to calculate the cost of the cocktail

1. identify the cost of the bottle used for the recipe.
2. identify the cost for ml by dividing the total cost of the bottle by ml.
3. identify the cost per portion used for the drink by multiplying the cost of 1 ml by the quantity used.
4. add the eventual cost of the garnish, ice, and even the cost of the glass if you like (we are not adding any of this time).

For example, let's take a Negroni with the following recipe:

Ingredient	Gin	Sweet vermouth	Bitter
Quantity used	30ml	30ml	30ml
£ Cost bottle	(700ml) = 17.65	(750ml) = 13.90	(700ml) = 15.95
£ Cost per ml	17.65: 700 = 0.025	13.90: 750 = 0.018	15.95: 700 = 0.022
£ Cost per quantity used	0.025 x 30 = £ 0.75	0.018 x 30 = £ 0.54	0.022 x 30 = 0.66
£ Total cost of cocktail	1.95		

Food and beverages pairing

I've been always fascinated by the science that is behind the pleasure you experience when you find so many aspects together in a simple food-drink pairing.

Pairing a drink with food is not something snobby; you were doing it since you were a child: enough to remember the cookies that you were dripping in the milk? Or the Cola with a slice of pizza?

Food and beverages are diverse and complex and the goal is to provide pleasure. Everybody can relate to the idea of the pleasure of eating or drinking something delicious. It's enjoying what we like and not what we don't. Certainly, there are so many factors that influence this experience, positively or negatively. The right drink can enhance a dining experience and the wrong drink can ruin an entire meal.

There is a science behind pairings that has to do with all sorts of factors from the environment, climate, temperature of the drink, of the dish, but also the environment, the emotional status of the person, culture, palate's taste, the ambience, the occasion, the season, the quality and aspect of the food and also the quality of the service, texture, regionally.

This concept can be applied not just for wine-food but also a pairing that consists of food and: water, spirits, coffee, tea, oil, and obviously cocktails.

You obtain a great result when the food chosen is paired with the drink in order to put both of them in evidence without fighting the other; the food makes the drink taste better and the drink makes the food taste better.

Pairing food and drink is not as simple as it was 20 or 30 years ago, when it was primarily a wine red or white or from Italy or France. Serve red wine with red meat is a classic but following the evolution of the cuisine, you must follow not just the primary ingredient but also the sauces/seasoning (porcini mushroom works fantastic with a big red, but if the mushrooms are chanterelle – dry white wine).

There has always been fear of drinking cocktails and mixed drinks with that 'high class' meal- or any meal for the matter.

There are some bits of advice and suggestions:
For sure it comes to your senses; let them guide your choices. Food and beverage pairing is all about listening to what your eyes, nose, mouth, and brain tell you. Think if you want to go for comfort or adventure. Unconventional combinations, why not? Consider the occasion as well.

Think regionally: if grows together, it goes together. If you go on a holiday in a specific region you will try their food and their drinks. Understanding regional pairing is such an important rule of the sommeliers. Thinking regionally can open your mind to new possibilities and it will be easier to pair as well. In the sake example, the Japanese drink fit Japanese cuisine. Tequila and Mexican inspired meal.

Consider body when pairing drinks, pay attention not only to flavour but also to the mouthfeel. For example, apple juice has a whole different body than tomato juice, which is different than seltzer. A full-bodied wine with dessert. It is the same for the cocktail. A full-bodied cocktail for the end of the meal.

Impact body and alcohol. Everything you eat and drink has an impact. The body, think of milk: light like skimmed milk, medium-bodied like a semi-skimmed, and a full-bodied like to a whole one or a cream. One thing that affects the body and the impact of wine and beer is the alcohol level. If the food is very delicate, consider choosing a lower alcohol drink to keep things in balance.

Texture. A dish's texture and temperature will also have a bearing on its perfect pairing. Crispy dishes are often fried, calling for a bubbly beverage such as champagne or other sparkling wine, or beer. Serve to refresh the palate.

The cooking technique affects the texture and temperature of a dish. Tuna can be served raw as sushi or hot off the grill, each had a different flavour, temperature, texture, and pairing implications.

The consistency of a cocktail also plays into pairing decisions. Thicker cocktails made with liqueurs generally don't go well with red meat or rich sauces. Frozen cocktails can overwhelm the palate, while carbonated cocktails pair well with full-flavored foods.

Brightness, acidity/sourness. One tool you have for picking drinks that go well with food is acidity. In a cocktail, this could come from lemon or lime juice, vinegar. Some wines have more bright acidity than others. In beers, brightness can come from hops that offer citrus or fruity character to the brew. Sour Belgian or Flemish style beers offer acidity in spades.

Acidity can contrast richness in your food, like a squeeze from a lemon wedge can help a plate of fried clams. Fat can coat your tongue, acidity can cleanse it and refresh your mouth. Use this tool to your advantage. For example with a salad, a Riesling because is a little sweet, has nice acidity, and is very fruity. Just like a Sidecar. Beer is low in acid so, for this reason, goes very well with a low spicy food.

The carbonation helps to clean the palate when you are eating a rich dish, refreshing your mouth for another bite.

Tannins in wine come from the skins, stems, seeds, or oak barrels. Tea has the same thing. In a big red wine, the tannins help the wine to go with meat, softening the fat and the protein. The fat and the protein help calm the harshness of the tannin.

With the spicy food, the tannins can accentuate their presence, so the pairing is not going to be great.

Sweetness is intended not just like cake or cookies but also the sauces that come with a main such as BBQ sauce, caramelized onion, etc. An off-dry wine or a beer with a touch of residual sugar and malty sweetness, will bring out the best in these dishes and not be overshadowed. The basic rule for pairing for dessert is to go sweeter with your drink than your food, as the sweetness in food increases the perception of bitterness, acidity, and the burning effect of the alcohol and at the same time decrease the perception of body, sweetness, and fruitiness in the drink. Dry champagne and wedding cake? Simply no!!!

On the opposite side, salty food will increase the perception of the body in drinks and decrease the perception of bitterness and acidity in the drinks.

The mix of sweet and salty is a subjective pleasure. One of my all-time favourites is blue cheese and sweet wine.

Umami. Glutamate and malt are found in the beer and work great with umami and earthy food flavours. Sherry- olive is an umami bomb and keep in mind that umami in food will increase the perception of bitterness, acidity and alcohol burn and will decrease the perception of body, sweetness, and fruitiness in the wine.

Consider richness. If you have a very rich dish you need a pretty rich drink that is full-bodied in style. How to measure richness? Simply by leaving the drink in the middle of your tongue and if you have a milky or creamy sensation mean is full-bodied; if is thin like the water is light-bodied.

Considering weight/volume when pairing. Like food, beverages have their volume or intensity.

Very important to wake up the palate nicely. Bear in mind the fact that the pairing should always follow what comes before and after a particular course. Just like you never start with pork and then move to a fish or a salad, we would never begin with a big brown spirit, stirred and strong, and then move to a light citrusy cocktail served tall.

Balance flavours. Pair to compare – pair a beverage with food that has a similar taste or textural characteristics, savouring the similarities between the two.

Remember that a drink can complement a dish by either matching or contrasting its flavour; enhance, don't compete.

Try not to think of beverages as complements to a meal, but as condiments like salt and pepper, olive oil, and vinegar.

Match the mixer. The prevailing flavour in most cocktails comes from the mixers, not the spirits. Keep this in mind when you are pairing. Make sure the mixer in the cocktail pair well with the key ingredient in the food. For instance, the lemon essence in a Margarita goes well with fresh seafood, like raw oysters.

Drinks like Martinis, Margaritas, and Cosmopolitans are best paired with foods that can soften the taste of alcohol. These foods include smoked fish or fried foods. Cheeses also soften the alcohol in spirits like cognac or scotch. When finishing a meal with cheese, pair with whiskey, cognac, or scotch because those smoky flavours can penetrate and cut through the fattiness and saltiness of the cheese.

Salad and high alcoholic drinks just don't mix.

Also, another very important factor to consider is the bitterness in food as increase the bitterness in the drink and the chili heat in food will increase the perception of bitterness, acidity and alcohol burn and decrease the perception of body, richness, sweetness, and fruitiness in the wine.

Sustainability

Working in a bar, a very important ingredient to consider is the concept of Sustainability, an aspect that focuses on meeting the needs of the present without compromising the ability of future generations to meet their needs and this concept is composed of three pillars: economic, environmental, and social.

See below some tips on how to be more sustainable:

Environment sustainability

- Say stop to plastic!
- No more plastic vacuum bag. Silicone reusable vacuum bag instead.
- Reuse is also sustainable! Don't throw away your juice. Instead use pickling for your pineapple, mandarin, or other juices to create exceptional alternatives to the classic citrus acidity.
- No more clingfilm. There are myriads of alternatives to it.
- No ore plastic straw. Use metal, glass, or paper as alternatives.
- Being sustainable means also to homegrown your celery, basil, and turmeric. So easy to do so.
- Waste is a resource. Create a delicious husk cordial with the leftover citrus.
- Reduce paper and postage and go technological.
- Using local ingredients to help to promote the local farmers. Just buy locally your celery, tomatoes, strawberries.

Keep in mind that sustainability goes hand in hand with seasonality.

As well as being a source of quality food, farmers' markets are good for the environment. Everything is produced locally, cutting down on food miles, so less road for the camion to reach your bar. And less road means less pollution. And less pollution means a better world.

- Minimize the amount of electricity you use by turning off lights when you leave a room. So simple and very effective on your electricity bill too.
- Create a coaster using the leftover corks or husks. They are fancy and last forever (almost).

Economic sustainability

- Sustainable is also from an economic and social point of view: fighting poverty, better education, are just two simple examples.

Social sustainability

- Promoting wellbeing. We know that we are working in an environment that requires immense physical and psychological effort. Look after yourself by practicing regular sports activities.
- Common goal: end hunger, achieve food security, and improved nutrition.
- Seems more an aspect of the past in the bar industry: gender discrimination, but sadly there are still happening similar episodes worldwide. Surely, we can fight this!
- Do not throw your clothes away! Donate! Do not throw your books away! Resell!

- When was your last time you have done some social work? Such as working with a local farmer. And of course, for free!
- The goal of sustainable development is to meet the needs of today, without compromising the needs of tomorrow. This means we cannot continue using current levels of resources as this will not leave enough for future generations. Stabilizing and reducing carbon emissions is key to living within environmental limits.
- Definitely, the next aspect is something that we can control much better: alcohol abuse. It also means sustainability.

Cocktails

Some very important information to keep in mind when creating cocktails:

- Prepare the garnish in advance so you can avoid letting the drink sit there while you are preparing your garnishes, to avoid over diluting and/or changing the drink's temperature.
- Have the glassware ready and make sure they are always cold before pouring the drink inside especially when is serving up. Exceptions are made obviously for the room temperature and hot drinks.
- When you have an order, I highly recommend starting with preparing the mise en place for the vessel where the drinks will be prepared and the way I like it is in the way I receive the order: the first drink ordered is the first on the left and then I build from the left to right.
- Then proceed with placing the cocktail's ingredients starting with the drops and dashes first as they have normally the smallest quantity, then follow with the less expensive ingredient, the amount, the density of the ingredients therefore the juices first, and the syrups afterward. Lastly the main spirit, then egg, creams, and then soft and sparkling drinks when need to top up.
- Ideally build all the drinks together so they can be served all together and as for the technique: stir first, then roll and throw, shake, build.
- I highly recommend touching each bottle once while building drinks as this will increase your speed.

This is diagram that I am using when creating drinks and I recommend you use it to give direction to the drinks!

Gin cocktails

Gin is an alcoholic beverage obtained by the distillation of a fermented wheat and barley in which macerates botanicals: a mixture of herbs, spices, plants and roots. Among these are juniper berries that characterize the scent and the taste. The name of the distillate comes from the names of juniper plants that produce berries.

Alaska
Alaska is a gin-based cocktail, with high alcohol content, and is probably the ultimate expression of a drink based on the herbal French liqueur, Chartreuse.

The diet of the Eskimos
In *The Savoy Cocktail Book* by Harry Craddock is listed but there nothing about its origins. For sure this exquisite potion does not constitute the basic diet of the Eskimos but was probably invented in South Carolina.

Ingredients
- 2 dashes of orange bitter
- 20 ml yellow Chartreuse
- 50 ml gin

How to make it
Pour all ingredients over ice in a mixing glass and stir. Serve in an iced cold cocktail glass.

Garnish
Lemon twist.

~~~~~~

Aviation

Aviation is a unique cocktail of charm and flavour, by a gentle delicacy that plays with the resinous tones of gin and the floral notes of the Violette liqueur, sweet complexity of the maraschino but balanced by the citrus presence.

In honour of...

The drink's invention is often attributed to Harry Craddock. He has the merit to published it in *The Savoy Cocktail Book* in 1930 without the presence of Crème de Violette.

The original recipe dates back to 1916, when Hugo Ensslin, the head bartender of the Wallick Hotel in New York, skilfully mixed gin, maraschino, fresh lemon juice, and Crème de Violette, a violet liqueur with an enchanting aroma that gives the drink a bluish colour of great charm and the drink is dedicated to the aviators of the WW 1.

Ingredients
- 20 ml lemon juice
- 5 ml Violette liqueur
- 10 ml maraschino
- 45 ml gin

How to make
Shake the ingredients together with ice. Strain and serve up into chilled glass.

Garnish
Garnish with a marasca cherry.

~~~~~~

Fortified Wines

Vermouth is a fortified wine – meaning a wine to which a distilled spirit, usually brandy is added, and heavily aromatised with herbs and botanicals. It must contain one of the three types of Artemisia: absinthium, pontica or maritima, to be called vermouth.

Sherry is a fortified wine made from white grapes that are grown near the town of Jerez in Andalusia, Spain.

The word Sherry is an anglicisation of Xeres and is produced with Palomino grapes, Pedro Ximenez and Muscatel.

Jerez (known with this name as well) was the first wine in Spain to which the Denominación de Origen was given – abbreviated as DO – whose area is bounded by the territories of the municipalities of Jerez de la Frontera, Sanlúcar de Barrameda and El Puerto de Santa María.

Port takes its name from the Portuguese city of Oporto, also known as Porto, which is a protected region or appellation since 1756, making it the 3rd oldest after Chianti (1716) and Toja (1730), which lies at the mouth of the Duoro River (in Portuguese means the Golden River) that is thrown into the Atlantic Ocean.

~~~~~~

Bijou
Crisp and herbaceous, the classic Bijou cocktail from the late 1800s blends gin with a bouquet of herbs and spice from Chartreuse and vermouth.

The jewel
Bijou means 'jewel' in French and was created by Harry Johnson. The reason for the name because contains the colours of the three jewels: diamond for gin, emerald for the green Chartreuse, and ruby for the sweet vermouth.

Ingredients
- 2 dashes of orange bitters   - 30 ml sweet vermouth
- 30 ml green Chartreuse   - 30 ml gin

How to make it
Pour all ingredients over ice in a mixing glass and stir. Serve in an iced cold cocktail glass.

Garnish
Orange twist.

Bramble
If you are looking for a cocktail with an elegant taste that can be drunk at all times, Bramble is for you and this is thanks to its simplicity, freshness and also its great visual effect, and fruity taste.

The bramble bush effect
The drink was created in 1980 by the cocktail guru Dick Bradsell in London and the reason for the name is because of the bramble bush effect.

Ingredients
- 25 ml lemon juice
- 12.5 ml sugar syrup
- 50 ml gin
- 10 ml blackberry liqueur float

How to make
Pour the ingredients in a shaker except for the blackberry liqueur. Shake and strain in an old-fashioned glass over crushed ice. Float the blackberry liqueur.

Garnish
Garnish with blackberries and lemon peel.

Try this:

You can make your own sugar syrup or you can buy it. Obviously, the second option is more expensive.

To make your own you can use equal parts water and sugar and my favourite recipe includes a mixture of 2 parts sugar beet to 1 part water, brought to nearly the boiling point and simmered for 5 minutes, also known as rich syrup or rock candy syrup, and the result has a richer taste. This is also the ratio used in this book for the cocktails. The sugar can be white, brown, coconut, demerara, or even a blend.

You can even replace the water with coconut water, grape juice, sugar cane juice, water from the tree such as maple tree water, cactus juice, and by doing so will change the texture of the final result.

I love adding a touch of Arabic gum (the dosage rate of Arabic gum powder is between 1% to 2%) to make it thicker and to have a better, richer, and more elastic texture (texture the longer it stays, the better texture it will have). This will be known as gum syrup and was a very common ingredient during the golden era of cocktails. Make sure to dissolve the powder, ideally by rehydrating in a bit of hot water by whisking for few seconds and let rest for 2-3 hours at room temperature. At this point, you can incorporate it into your warm syrup and mix.

Then you can add some dry citrus zest to gives more freshness and vanilla pods for a better complexity (everyone loves vanilla as is associated with mother's milk: it is warm, gentle and pleasant).

I also suggest measuring by weight rather than volume as you will be more accurate.

~~~~~~

Chaplin Cocktail

From one of the most important hotels in New York, Walford Astoria Hotel, a cocktail was created and dedicated to a legend of the entertainment world: Charlie Chaplin.

The Waldorf-Astoria

The Waldorf-Astoria is one of the most important and luxurious hotels in the Big Apple, if not the world. No one would have imagined in 1890 that the feud between two rich cousins would have created one of the most enduring names in the hotel industry in the world.

In 1893, William Waldorf Astor, from the ashes of his home, on the corner of 5th Avenue and 33rd Street, built a hotel, which was designed by the famous architect Henry Hardenbergh. Four years later, his cousin John Jacob Astor IV, one of the *Titanic*'s survivors in 1912, had a new building built on his adjacent property, housing a prestigious hotel to which he named Astoria Hotel. At the end of the family hostility, the two hotels were connected by a corridor and the complex took the name Waldorf = Astoria (the double line, later removed, meant the passage between the two buildings). In the spring of 1929, the entire complex was ceded to the Empire State Corporation, the company that built the Empire State Building, the art deco-style skyscraper of the city, after the demolition of the old structure.

Ingredients
- 30 ml lime
- 5 ml sugar syrup
- 30 ml apricot brandy
- 30 ml gin

How to make it
Place all the ingredients in a shaker, add ice and shake. Serve up in a cocktail glass.

Garnish
Garnish with a lime twist and discard.

Clover Club

Thanks to its splendid aromatic qualities and elegant taste, the Clover Club is a drink that can be enjoyed at all hours.

The men's club

The history of the Clover Club is relatively recent, it was born in the early 1900s in the US, and pre-dates Prohibition, and takes its name from the Philadelphia men's club with which it shares the name.

Ingredients
- 5 fresh raspberries
- 20 ml lemon juice
- 5ml sugar syrup
- 15 ml raspberry liqueur
- 45 ml gin
- 15 ml egg white

I will confess that I am not a big fan of egg white in cocktails and I am always using different alternatives and my favourite alternative is perhaps using 3 drops of soapbark instead of 15ml egg white and I highly recommend using it.

How to make it

Muddle the raspberries in a shaker and add the remaining ingredients. Dry shake, add ice and shake vigorously for few extra moments. Double strain in a cocktail glass.

Garnish

Garnish with edible flowers.

~~~~~~

Corpse Reviver 2

The Corpse Reviver no2 is a historic cocktail and be described as a concert of elegance.

How to revive a body...

The Corpse Reviver cocktails family are intended as 'hair of the dog' hangover cures, hence the name. Hair of the dog takes the name from a practice from Scotland to treat dog bite by placing hair of the dog in the bite wound.

Most of the Corpse Reviver cocktails have been lost to time, but this one survived and is really request as well.

Harry Craddock, head bartender at the American Bar at the Savoy, mentioned in *The Savoy Cocktail Book*, 1930 edition.

Ingredients

- 2 dashes absinthe
- 20 ml lemon juice
- 20 ml triple sec
- 20 ml vermouth (Lillet)
- 20 ml gin

How to make

Pour all ingredients in a shaker and after a good shake strain in a chilled Martini glass.

Garnish

Squeeze the essential oils from a lemon peel and garnish with it.

French 75

The French 75 is a classic aperitif cocktail, a delicious drink that concentrates freshness and minerality. It is part of the family of sparkling and this is due to a touch of luxury with the Champagne presence.

Accuracy and speed

It is believed that Scot Harry MacElhone (owner of Harry's American Bar in Paris), invented and named the drink in 1926. The inspiration for the title was apparently a 75mm Howitzer field gun used by the French and the Americans in World War 1. The gun was known for its accuracy and speed, and the French 75 is said to have such a kick that it felt like being hit by just such a weapon.

Very interesting that Harry MacElhone never claimed the drink as his own, though, instead citing McGarry of Buck's Club in London as drink's father.

For sure *The Savoy Cocktail Book* played an important role had not in inventing the drink, but in popularising it. Once printed, it spread across the Atlantic and was served up in New York's infamous Stork Club, thus cementing its place as an icon.

Ingredients

- 15 ml lemon juice   - 10 ml sugar syrup
- 30 ml gin   - top champagne (approx. 60ml)

How to make

Shake all the ingredients except champagne. Strain into a flute glass and top up with champagne.

Garnish

Garnish with a cherry.

~~~~~~

Gibson
Brother with the Dry Martini and they share the same ingredients and the same ratio but what makes really sensational and very unique a Gibson?

The Gibson Girls
The Gibson is believed to have been created by San Francisco businessman Walter D.K. Gibson in the late 1800s thought that eating onions prevented colds, hence the addition of the mini allium.

But the most popular story said that Charles Dana Gibson – an American artist who created the Gibson Girls (fashionable ideal girls of the late 19th century and early 20th century) – challenged a bartender to improve the Martini recipe. The bartender made a Martini and serve it with pickled onion and named after the patron.

In the 1959 film *North by Northwest* by Alfred Hitchcock, there is a scene in the 20th Century Limited train where the actor Roger Thornhill, in the dining car train orders a Gibson.

Ingredients
- 10 ml vermouth dry
- 60 ml gin

How to make it
Pour the ingredients into a mixing glass and stir until ice cold. Serve in a Martini glass.

Garnish
Pickled onion.

Try this: House fortified wine
I love using this unique house blend as is more complex and has some wonderful mineral notes and you can too replicate or perhaps create your house fortified wine by mixing different fortified wines and my favourite dry option involves using

a mix of vermouths from France and Italy and in addition another fortified Spanish wine: fino sherry.

Gimlet

The Gimlet was promoted and drunk by British officers back in the 19th Century. Citrus juice was a gift from the Gods to sailors, as it prevented them from catching scurvy – a brutal, painful, and sometimes deadly disease brought about by vitamin C deficiency.

The Limeys

Rear-Admiral Sir Thomas Desmond Gimlette (served 1879–1913) is cited by some as the namesake of the Gimlet. Acting as a doctor to sailors, he administered gin with lime in order to mask the bitter taste. Allegedly, he introduced this to his shipmates to help them swallow down the lime juice as an anti-scurvy medication.

British sailors, though – unlike their superior Naval officers – had rum rations, and so used to mix this in with their lime. The drink became known as 'grog', and so great was their consumption of this 'medicine' that sailors soon became known as 'Limeys'.

Another credible etymological story is that the concoction was named after the hand tool, which was used to bore into barrels of spirits on Navy ships – a gimlet.

Rose's Lime Cordial has played a central role in the story of the Gimlet, as it was the accessible and necessary sweet fruit preserve of choice by sailors. The cordial was first produced by Scottish entrepreneur Lauchlan Rose in 1867 and was the world's first fruit concentrate. Rose patented the process in a move that quickly paid off, as later that year a law was passed that all vessels should carry lime juice and serve it as a daily ration to their crews.

The cocktail was featured in Harry Craddock's 1930 *The Savoy Cocktail Book*, where he offered the advice that the drink "can be iced if desired."

Ingredients
- 15 ml lime cordial
- 60 ml gin

How to make it
Stir all ingredients over ice in a mixing glass and serve in an old-fashioned glass on ice or straight up.

Garnish
Lime twist and discard.

Try this: Bergamot cordial

- 200 ml water	- 4 g malic acid
- 125 g sugar	- 2 g tartaric acid
- 4–6 g dry bergamot peel	- 1 g ascorbic acid
- ½ vanilla pod	- 2 g salt

Dissolve the sugar, acids, and salt in water. Pour in a vacuum bag and add the bergamot peel, jasmine, and vanilla. Remove the air, seal, and vacuum cook for two hours at 60°C.

Let rest for 12 hours. Strain and bottle.

You can add a touch of alcohol so in this way your cordial will be preserved for longer. The original cordial recipes were including the use of spirit for the same reason earlier mentioned.

If you are a bitter lover and you go crazy for the gin you might consider also the **Pink Gin** cocktail. It was created by the members of the Royal Navy around 1850, to make the consumption of bitters more palatable, as it was used as a treatment for seasickness.

James Bond, in the novel of 1965, *The Man with the Golden Gun* orders a Pink Gin cocktail with Beefeater and plenty of bitters, while in Jamaica.

- 6 dashes Angostura bitter
- 60 ml gin

Stir the ingredients over ice and serve in a cocktail glass or even in an old fashioned on rocks.

No garnish needed for this drink.

~~~~~~

Gin Fizz

Back to 1770

The Gin Fizz is one of the oldest cocktails in the history of drinks and we find it already noted in the recipe book of Jerry Thomas, the bible of cocktails: *How to Mix Drinks or The Bon-Vivant's Companion* and according to some its recipe dates back to 1750 and is a variant of Gin Tonic.

At this point, we can say that is very similar to a John Collins, but first of all, in John, you find two drops of Angostura and is a cocktail that is built, while the Gin Fizz is shaken.

A recipe for a John Collins is featured in the *Steward 1869 Barkeeper's Manual* and believed that the drink takes the name of its creator: a headwaiter who was working in a restaurant bar in Mayfair, in London.

Some years later, in 1876, following the use of Old Tom Gin, the name changed to Tom Collins.

Ingredients
- 25 ml lemon juice
- 12.5ml sugar
- 50 ml gin (use an Old Tom gin for a Tom Collins or even tequila for a Mexican Collins)
- top soda water
- 2 dashes of Angostura bitter on top (for the John Collins)

How to make it
Shake and serve over ice in a highball the Gin Fizz and top up with the soda.

Build directly in a highball glass over ice the John Collins and the Tom Collins.

Garnish
Lemon wedge and marasca cherry.

There are other variants of the Gin Fizz:
Golden Fizz-egg yolk added.
Silver Fizz- egg white.
Royal Fizz- entire egg.

Hanky Panky

When it comes to cocktails, the Hanky Panky is the quintessence of elegance. It is a historic cocktail and it is often described as a flag of the America bar at the Savoy since the drink it was created there a long time ago and still enjoyed and know worldwide.

The Hanky Panky falls into the category of the pre-dinner drinks, or those drinks prepared by an aperitif accent, in order to stimulate your appetite but also perfect as an all-day drink due to its charming taste. Considering also the heavy alcohol content and the presence and qualities of the Fernet Branca, this drink is also an ideal candidate as an after-dinner drink.

The drink was created in the early 1900s by Ada 'Colley' Coleman at the Savoy's American Bar in London for the actor and producer Sir Charles Hawtrey. Ada said that she spent hours experimenting with cocktails until she invented this creation and when Charles tasted exclaimed: "By Jove, this is a real hanky panky."

Ingredients
- 7.5 ml Fernet Branca
- 40 ml vermouth sweet
- 40 ml gin

How to make it
Pour the ingredients into a mixing glass and stir until ice cold. Serve straight up.

Garnish
Orange twist and discard and a cherry.

Try this: Aeropress earl grey gin
Using the Aeropress you can create a fabulous gin infuse earl grey in few seconds without adding the bitter element of it but just the aroma.

Last Word
The Last Word is an aromatic drink thanks to the 130 herbs of which the green Chartreuse is made, a sweet green liqueur produced by the Carthusian monks in the Chartreuse monastery, from which it takes its name.

It is also fruity and sweet thanks to the presence of maraschino (sweet liqueur of Dalmatian origin based on visciole cherries or sour cherries), but perfectly balanced by the presence of the citrus part.

A famous exponent

This is a Prohibition-era cocktail (probably 1916) developed at the Detroit Athletic Club and it seems that it was mixed for the first time for Frank Fogarty, a famous exponent of the theatrical genre Vaudeville, a genre of a brilliant and very witty comedy of French origin very popular at the beginning of the 20th century.

The first printed appearance in 1951 in the cocktail book *Bottoms Up!* by Ted Saucier. The reason for the name probably because its creator was usually saying: 'The Last Word' before closing his exhibition.

Ingredients
- 20 ml lemon juice
- 20 ml maraschino
- 20 ml Green Chartreuse
- 20 ml gin

How to make it
Place all the ingredients in a shaker, add ice, shake and strain in a cocktail glass. Garnish and serve.

Garnish
Garnish with a marasca cherry.

Try this: Clarified effervescent Last Word Punch on the rocks
Using the milk punch idea that consists of using milk – citrus juice combination, in order to have a clear drink and a very distinctive taste and texture.

In the Jerry Thomas' Bartenders Guide: *How to Mix Drinks or The Bon Vivant's Companion*, published in 1862, there is a recipe of an English Milk Punch, which consist of a mixture of lemon rind, sugar, pineapple, cloves, coriander, cinnamon, brandy, rum arrack, green tea, and boiling water, and the method suggest that all the ingredients to be steeped for six hours, before adding lemon juice and hot milk and then filter through a jelly bag until "the punch has passed bright."

For our clarified effervescent Last Word Punch, use the same ingredients as above but in addition, add 50 ml whole milk (you can even use other milk alternatives such as vegetal milk and you can even produce your vegetable milk.). Ideal is to make this drink in big batches.

Let rest in the fridge overnight and strain using a cheesecloth the next day.

At this point pour it into the soda stream bottle, add 10 ml water that normally will come from the dilution, and carbonate several times making sure to release the pressure between carbonation circles.

Pour over ice, squeeze the essential oils from a lime peel, discard and serve.

How to make your vegetable milk

Milk is a white-coloured drink and from a chemical point of view, it is an emulsion of oil in water and is often referred to as an animal derived drink. Vegetable milk is a great alternative as it is free of casein, lactose, and cholesterol and therefore is also suitable for those who have allergies, intolerances, vegans or simply prefer this taste.

To make it is very simple: You can use oat, walnut, coconut, quinoa, etc. and my favourite is almond milk: rinse and soak them water overnight, blend until smooth, strain through a cheesecloth, add a touch of thickening agent. sugar, salt, some vanilla flavours and ready to go.

Long Island Iced Tea

This drink is very well-known around the world and highly requested for its potential yet aromatic character.

The story goes as this drink have been invented around the 1920s during Prohibition in the United States by an 'Old Man Bishop' in a local community named Long Island in Kingsport in Tennessee and later the drink was perfected by Ransom Bishop, Old Man Bishop's son.

A very interesting and funny mention goes to the fact the people were drinking this concoction even in front of the police while Prohibition was in place as the taste and smell was masked and looking very similar to an iced tea – hence the name too.

Ingredients

- 30 cl lemon juice
- 15 ml sugar syrup
- 15 ml triple sec
- 15 ml tequila
- 15 ml vodka
- 15 ml white rum
- 15 ml gin
- Top with cola

How to make it

Place the ingredients in a shaker except for the cola, add ice, shake and strain in a highball glass. Finish with the cola. Garnish and serve.

Garnish

Garnish with a lemon peel and mint spring.

Variations

- Grateful Dead, known also as the Purple Rain – which uses the same mix as a Long Island but the Triple Sec is replaced with a shot of Chambord and the cola replaced with lemon soda.

- The Adios Motherfu***r: Blue Curaçao substituting the Triple Sec and lemon soda substituting the cola.
- Long Beach Iced Tea: cranberry juice instead of cola.
- Tokyo Iced Tea: Midori instead of Coca-Cola.

Martinez

The Martinez is more than a cocktail: is a masterpiece, a concentrate of aromatic flavours. Sweeter and more delicate than a Martini Dry and due to its roundness, it is a cocktail suitable for all hours, both as an aperitif and after dinner.

The legend says...

It is believed that Martinez is the father of the Martini cocktail, and the legend says that the name Martinez comes from the Californian city of the same name, in which the bartender Julio Richelieu served a special drink to a miner, and he called it Martinez.

The original recipe comes from around 1884 and was based on *Dutch genever*. Thanks to Jerry Thomas and his famous *How to Mix Drinks or The Bon-Vivant's Companion* the drink became widely popular.

Ingredients

- 2 dashes of orange bitter
- 15 ml sweet vermouth
- 15 ml dry vermouth
- 10 ml maraschino liqueur
- 45 ml old tom gin

How to make

Stir the drink over ice and serve in a chilled Martini glass.

Garnish

Squeeze the essential oils from an orange peel and discard. Finish with a marasca cherry.

Try this: Martinez pods using the reverse spherification
With the following recipe, you can make about 6 Martinez pods

- 2 dashes of orange bitter
- 15 ml sweet vermouth
- 15 ml dry vermouth
- 10 ml maraschino liqueur
- 45 ml old tom gin
- 30 ml water
- 2.3 g calcium lactate gluconate (2% of the cocktail weight)

Add all ingredients to a small bowl and mix with the help of a blender.

Let rest to avoid bubbles in your pods.

Pour the mixture into an ice cube tray, place in the freezer, and freeze.

At this point prepare your sodium alginate bath:

- 5 g sodium alginate
- 1 litre distilled water

Mix these two ingredients with a blender and let rest for around 24 hours to allow the bubbles to disappear. After the resting period, gently warm the sodium alginate bath to around 50°C, and in addition prepare two extra containers with cold water.

Add the frozen cocktail pod into the sodium alginate bath and stir gently around the pod, making sure to not touching the pod until the membrane has formed.

At this point, with the help of a perforated spoon, transfer the pod to the first cold water bath making sure to don't transfer any sodium alginate mixture.

Rinse thoroughly by stirring the water and repeat this process with the second bath.

Serve them on a tray and the great aspect of this process is that you can store the pods in a jar. Make sure that is filled with the cocktail liquid without the calcium.

Martini

Martini is definitely more than a cocktail and behind that elegant, clear ice-cold drink there is a lot of mystery. Let's discover some of its secrets.

A journey back in time

The Martini has been always a fascinating drink and gains its popularity due to its mystery. Regarding its birth, there is a mention in 1776, where a French musician (by German origins), Jean Paul Martini Schwarzedorf was always enjoying his favourite drink that was made with genievre and dry white wine. The other musicians and artists requested this fantastic drink and what for him become the 'usual' drink for others became Martini's drink.

The story that is more plausible comes from 1888, from one of the greatest bartender ever, Harry Johnson, from his bestseller *Bartender's Manual*, where he added not an only illustration but also contained detailed instruction of a drink called Martinez: same as Manhattan but with gin instead of whiskey. And from here comes the fact that Martinez is the father of the Martini.

Where does that olive come from?

There are two stories regarding this:

- A young French man, called Julio Richelieu, moved to Martinez, California, and decided to open a bar in Ferry Street where he was mixing and serving a drink with a green olive that was called Martinez around 1870. The people of Martinez claim that the namesake Martinez cocktail was first produced in their town and there is even a plaque that commemorates its creation.
- Around 1910, a young Italian emigrant bartender called Martini from Arma di Taggia (in the northwest of Italy) made a gin and vermouth concoction and served it with olive for the millionaire John Rockefeller. Rockefeller was so impressed by this drink that he asked for its name. The young bartender suggested to be called after his guest, it was obvious because it was created for him but then Rockefeller decided to call after its creator: Martini.

Ingredients

There are many variants, but the ingredients are always three:

- gin or vodka
- vermouth dry
- garnish.

Following the ingredients that you use is going to affect the drink either in a great way or even in a really bad way. This is down to the gin or the vodka (but can be used even both and you have a Vesper Martini), the vermouth, and also the quality of the ice, that must be clear and healthy.

Garnish

The presence of the lemon twist as a garnish adds that citrus touch due to its essential oils when squeezed. If you prefer savoury go for an olive. The Nocellara are my favourites but you can try also anchovies stuffed olives or blue cheese stuffed ones. Simply delicious!

We can argue for days which are the most indicative olives for a Martini but all of us know that the Nocellara are great candidates for the podium, for their crisp texture and balanced buttery yet clean taste. There is no substitute for quality therefore invest in some that come from Valle del Belice in the southwest of Sicily.

To be considered!!!

There are also people that they are considered 'purists' and for this reason, they prefer not to garnish at all their drink. The reason is that they love the pure flavour and taste of that drink that they don't need any garnish.

Recipe

- 10 ml vermouth dry   - 60 ml gin/vodka

If you prefer:

Naked – no vermouth at all.
Extra dry – use 5 ml vermouth dry.
Wet – 20 ml vermouth dry.

For a Direct Martini, place your spirit, gin or vodka, in a freezer and serve directly in a cocktail glass. Garnish and serve. The secret also here is that the spirit must be iced cold.

How to make it

Start by chilling your mixing glass and pour over ice the vermouth first and then the spirit you prefer. Stir until is ice cold and serve in a chilled Martini glass.

You can try also the Montgomery variation. The great Ernest Hemingway named the variation after Field Marshall Bernard Law Montgomery leader of the British Eight Army, during the Second World War's North African campaign, and the story goes that he would attack the German field Erwin Rommel – called the Desert Fox – and his men, only if His Majesty's forces outnumbered this formidable foe by 15:1 ratio.

~~~~~~~~~~~~~~~~~~~~~~~~~~~~~~~

Negroni

One of the most famous drinks in the world, appreciated for its bitter thirst-quenching, it is absolutely perfect for any occasion.

The Negroni count

Negroni, a drink by an aperitif profile, it was created in 1919 at the Caffè Cassoni bar in Florence by the bartender Fosco Scarselli for the Count Camillo Negroni. The count asked the bartender to change the soda water from his Americano cocktail with gin to commemorate his journeys in England. The drink was named after his patron.

Ingredients
- 30 ml Campari bitter
- 30 ml sweet vermouth
- 30 ml gin

Replace the gin with vodka and you'll have a Negroski; add sparkling wine instead of gin to have a Negroni sbagliato.

How to make
Part of the build-up family drinks but it can be also stirred. Serve in an old-fashioned glass with ice.

Garnish
Garnish with an orange peel or in a traditional way with an orange slice.

Try this:
Add 2 dashes of saline solution to your Negroni.

The presence of saline solution is vital for various reasons:

- To enhance the flavour of this specific combination of ingredients.
- Counteract bitter – it is often used to 'de-bitter'.
- Salt will also help release certain molecules in the food and drinks, bringing out some of the ingredients' flavours and making the final result more aromatic.
- Colour enhancer as the presence of the salt helps promote the drink s vibrant colour.
- Lower the temperature of the drinks when mixing.

Try this: Strawberry Campari
Infuse 500ml Campari with 250 g strawberries overnight at room temperature in order to have a glorious interpretation of the Negroni cocktail.

Drunken strawberry leather
Once the infusion is complete, strain the strawberries, add a spoon of olive oil, a pinch of citric acid, and a pinch of salt, blend all together and place on a baking foil and then in the dehydrating machine at 60°C for 6–8 hours.

Once dry but still must have an elastic, leathery feeling, cut into pieces and you can use it to garnish your cocktails.

Americano is another great Italian creation. Made with Campari bitter, sweet vermouth and soda. There are two theories regarding its name: takes its name from its bitter taste (amaricante in Italian) or the cocktail would be named in honour of Primo Carnera, an Italian boxer who was very active in the United States around 1930, and for this reason, he was called 'the American' (Americano in Italian), an invalid theory since the first mention of the drink dates back to about 1860.

Ramos Gin Fizz

Ramos Gin Fizz is a historic cocktail, one of the first invented and to become an icon and trend phenomenon, from the golden days of New Orleans cocktail era, and in fact, it is also known as New Orleans Gin Fizz.

The Shaking Team

Henry C. Ramos, bartender of the Meyer restaurant in New Orleans is credited with the invention of this sumptuous milky cocktail, with a harmless appearance, but with a seductive, aromatic, and fascinating taste. The story goes that a team of 20 bartenders were used only in the preparation of this drink as there was need to shake the Ramos for 12 minutes.

This drink is basically a Gin Fizz, made with gin, lime and lemon juice, soda, and with the addition of the other ingredients, the result is a velvety dream cocktail, full of floral notes and spicy gin flavour suggestions.

Ingredients

- 2 drops of vanilla extract
- 3 drops of orange flower water
- 12.5 ml lemon juice
- 12.5 ml lime juice
- 12.5 ml sugar syrup
- 50 ml fresh cream
- 45 ml gin
- 15 ml egg white
- soda to top up

How to make

Pour all the ingredients, apart from the soda, in a shaker and shake vigorously for 1 minute: cream and egg white must be mixed to perfection, so do not rush.

Now open the shaker and put some ice and shake for 1–2 minutes. It depends on how much you can resist!

Strain into a highball glass, add a bit of soda at the time and garnish if desired.

~~~~~~

Singapore Sling

The Singapore Sling is one of the most important and complex cocktails. Born as a simple pink cocktail for ladies, it becomes in a very short time a trendy cocktail, so that all the gentlemen now want it.

From Singapore with love

The creator of Singapore Sling is the legendary bartender Ngiam Tong Boon, bartender of the Raffles Hotel in Singapore, in whose museum the book with the original cocktail recipe is still kept and is a variant on the Gin Sling. The earliest published by Harry Craddock in *The Savoy Cocktail Book*.

There are a lot of ingredients used (8) to make this drink but the result worth it: a unique taste, complex, full of aromas and a thousand nuances, but at the same time fresh, dry with an extraordinary drinkability.

Ingredients
- 2 dashes of Angostura bitter
- 25 ml lemon juice
- 10 ml grenadine syrup
- 100 pineapple juice
- 7.5 ml Dom Benedictine
- 7.5 ml triple sec
- 15 ml Cherry Heering
- 30 ml gin

How to make it

Place all the ingredients in a shaker and shake vigorously. Strain in a highball over ice, garnish and serve.

Garnish

Garnish with dry pineapple and marasca cherry.

109

~~~~~~

Tuxedo

You have the Martinez which is the father of the Martini and then you have the Tuxedo which is believed to be the father of Martinez.

Put your jacket on

The Tuxedo cocktail is a drink of great aromatic complexity, gin base, dry vermouth with a few drops of orange bitter, absinthe, and the sweet touch of the maraschino.

The birthplace of the Tuxedo is credited to be The Tuxedo Club, a club for wealthy American gentlemen, which opened in 1886 but the drink appeared was at the beginning of 1900. For sure it was at the Club that the tuxedo jacket was originated – which was used to preserve clothes from tobacco smoke, made famous by the Prince of Wales.

Ingredients

- 3 dashes orange bitter
- 2.5 ml absinth
- 5 ml maraschino
- 30 ml dry vermouth
- 30 ml gin (I like to use an Old Tom gin for this drink)

How to make it

Pour all the ingredients in a mixing glass over ice and stir. Pour in a cocktail glass, garnish and serve.

Garnish

Garnish with an orange twist.

~~~~~~

Vesper Martini

The Vesper Martini is synonymous with James Bond. And like any curiosity that has James Bond as the protagonist, the origins of the drink are in a woman: Vesper, the first Bond Girl created by Ian Fleming.

Shaken not stirred!

The Vesper is a great cocktail, a variant of the Martini cocktail invented by the writer Ian Fleming and found in the 1953 novel *Casino Royale*, where the legendary James Bond expressly ask how to make and serve the drink: "In a deep champagne goblet. Three shots of Gordon's, one of vodka and a half measure of Kina Lillet. Shake it very well until it's ice-cold, then add a large slice of lemon peel."

It is named after a member of the same team – agent Vesper Lynd. Vesper in Latin means evening and she even mentioned that she "was born in a stormy evening."

The true Vesper Martini of James Bond is very difficult to reproduce, as today Lillet no longer produces that vermouth (Kina Lillet), so in the official recipe these days it is usual to use Lillet Blanc, very fragrant vermouth that is quite the opposite of the original, too sweet to be dry vermouth.

Ingredients
- 7.5 ml dry vermouth
- 15 ml vodka
- 45 ml gin

How to make
With this drink, we go against the rules because following its ingredients should be stirred but needs to be shaken following its origins.

Strain in a chilled Martini glass and garnish.

Garnish
Squeeze the essential oils from a lemon peel and use it as a garnish.

White Lady

This beautiful and elegant drink is believed to have been created by the bartender Harry MacElhone at Ciro's Club in London in 1919 and originally made with crème de menthe.

Harry Craddock (former head bartender at the American Bar and author of *The Savoy Cocktail Book*, 1930 edition) changed it with gin, and later another legendary bartender, Peter Dorelli, added the egg white.

Ingredients
- 25 ml lemon juice
- 25 ml triple sec
- 50 ml gin
- 15 ml egg white

How to make it
Add all the ingredients in a shaker without ice, then with ice, and strain in a cocktail glass. Serve without garnish but some essential oils from a lemon twist might be a great idea to break all the big bubbles on top of the drink and to add a citrus note to the drink.

Garnish
A favourite personal touch is to use some edible gold and strawberry extract just to add a new wonderful dimension to the drink.

Vodka cocktails

Vodka is a typical drink of Eastern European countries with crystal clear transparency, a very fine taste and a slight aroma; it is usually obtained from the distillation of cereals especially rye and wheat, but it is also possible to obtain it from other substances such as molasses, potatoes and other plants.

~~~~~~

Black Russian
Another great drink that wins not just for its simplicity but also for its fragrant and aromatic ingredient coffee liqueur, which mixed with vodka that acts as pilar for this drink.

The alternative dessert
You can drink Black Russian as a meditation drink for after dinner and as an alternative to a dessert try the White Russian.

This cocktail was created by Gustave Tops, bartender at the Bruxelles Metropole Hotel in 1949, for the American Ambassador in Luxembourg, Pearl Mesta.

Ingredients
- 30 ml coffee liqueur
- 40 ml vodka

For the White Russian float the cream on top.

For the Lebowski style mix the cream with all the ingredients.

How to make
Part of the build-up family drinks but it can be also stirred. Serve in an old-fashioned glass with ice.

Garnish
Garnish the White Russian with some grated chocolate.

Try this:
I am a big fan of cold brew coffee as is less acidic, less bitter, and has a smothering taste and I will share with you how to make a homemade cold brew coffee recipe. Obviously keep in mind that a lot of factors will affect the final result such as beans used and griding size, steeping time, temperature, dilution.

The ratio I am using is 4 to 1 and that means 4 cups of water to 1 cup grounded Arabica coffee.

Combine the ground coffee with water, then let it steep from 14 to 24 hours in the refrigerator in a closed jar. During this time, the coffee slowly infuses into the water, creating a strong, concentrated brew and if the result is more bitter than it would have, is ok to dilute with some extra water.

Once the steeping is done, you'll need to strain the coffee grounds out of the water and thin paper coffee filters do the job magnificently: simply place the coffee filter into a small fine-mesh sieve over a liquid measuring cup and pour the concentrate through it and the gravity will do its magic.

And if you want to make your cold brew coffee liqueur, for 1 litre, add and dissolve 200 g demerara sugar in 100 ml water in a pot by bringing it to boil.

Let cool and then add 525 ml of cold brew coffee, 1 vanilla bean, and 275ml vodka (or your favourite spirit), in order to have a liqueur with a 20% abv approx.

Allow the mixture to rest for 2 days, then remove the vanilla pod, bottle and keep in the fridge for up to 1 month.

Bloody Mary

Bloody Mary is a really delicious cocktail. Its fiery red colour is unique; warm and velvety, but with a spicy aftertaste, which makes the perfect cocktail for the hot summer afternoons as for the cold winter evenings and also to consider that is the king of the cure for the hangover. But why?

Hair of the dog

Fernand Petiot claimed to have invented the Bloody Mary in 1921 at the New York bar in Paris, a famous bar, frequented by Ernest Hemingway and the bar is also associated with the birth of the Sidecar cocktail.

The name of the drink is associated with Queen Mary 1ˢᵗ of England, nicknamed Bloody Mary as she was executing protestants in an attempt to re-establish the Catholic Church in England around 1550.

The drink is part of the hangover family know as well as the 'hair of the dog'. Hair of the dog is an antique Scottish remedy to cure the dog's bite by placing hair of the dog on the bite, so the idea of the Bloody Mary is to work in the same way.

Technically, it is not removing ethanol or any congener from your body, but makes you feel better – or less worse – and this is because the components are meant to release endorphins to calm down the pain.

It was known as well with the name of Red Snapper as it is less 'offensive' as a name, however in the current days with this name is intended the gin-based version.

Ingredients

- 4 dashes tabasco
- 20 ml lemon juice
- 20 ml Worcestershire sauce
- 80 ml of tomato juice
- 40 ml of vodka
- 5 ml fino sherry (personal touch)
- 1 bar spoon horseradish sauce
- salt and pepper

How to make it

Regarding the preparation method, you can build it or even using the spectacular rolling or throwing technique. Must take into consideration the thickness of your tomato juice so you can use the correct mixing technique.

Strain into a highball glass filled with ice.

Garnish

Garnish with a stick of celery, olive, and a grind of black pepper.

Try this:

As for the garnish, you can be also more innovative: in this case, we have created some fabulous tomato chips by blending tomato with a pinch of salt and pepper and then dehydrate. On top a touch of truffle sauce and a capper.

Try this:

You can incorporate different herbs and spices in order to create your personal spicy mix. Obviously, keep in mind possible allergies that you might add to your mix.

~~~~~~~~~~~~~~~~~~~~~~~~~~~~~~~~

Caesar

A Bloody Mary with Caesar mix – which is a blend of tomato juice and clam broth. It was created in 1969 by the restaurant manager Walter Chell in Calgary, Alberta, Canada. The inspiration is from the Venetian dish 'spaghetti alle vongole'. Since 2009 there is every year, the Caesar celebration day on May 13th.

~~~~~~

Bull shoot
Essentially is a Bloody Mary with beef bullion instead of tomato juice. Created around 1950 in the US.

~~~~~~

Cosmopolitan
The Cosmopolitan cocktail is a great American classic, often present in the social evenings for its taste characterized by the unmistakable sweet and dry union. In fact, the sour presence, given by the lime and cranberry juice, goes perfectly with the sweetness and the presence of the triple sec and the citrus and powerful presence of the vodka citron, transforming the cocktail into an enveloping mix.

A star is born
The origin of the Cosmopolitan is disputed. It is widely believed that the drink was created independently by different bartenders since the beginning of the 1900s and there are tales that attributing the birth of this drink even in the 17th century.

For sure the Cosmopolitan gained popularity in the 1990s when becoming a great protagonist in cinematography: its biggest role is in fact in the TV series *Sex and the City*, where the protagonist Carrie Bradshaw (interpreted by Sarah Jessica Parker) often sipped this cocktail.

It is not only in television that Cosmo (often called) has influenced popular culture but also in cosmetics: there is even a Cosmopolitan perfume.

Ingredients
- 15 ml lime juice
- 15 ml cranberry juice
- 15 ml triple sec
- 45 ml vodka citron

How to make it
Prepare in the shaker and serve in a cocktail glass previously chilled.

Garnish
Flaming orange twist.

~~~~~~~~~~~~~~~~~~~~~
Espresso Martini
The Espresso Martini is a delicious drink that lends very well to be drunk as an after-dinner, especially if accompanied by great friends, laughs, and sweets.

The young lady
Espresso Martini's recipe is very simple and should be served in a frozen cup. The vodka gives consistency and structure to the cocktail but does not add any flavour, moreover, there is no need, the mixture is already satisfying and has an enveloping taste.

As for its birth, it was created by a legendary bartender, Dick Bradsell, in the late 1980s, while at the Brasserie Soho in London for a young lady who asked a drink that would "Wake me up, and then f**k me up."

Ingredients
- 10 ml sugar syrup
- 1 freshly made espresso coffee (approx. 30ml)
- 10 ml of coffee liqueur
- 50 ml of vodka

How to make
Pour all the ingredients in a cocktail shaker with an ice cube and shake vigorously for a good amount of time. Strain in a cold coupe glass.

Garnish
Take care of the look of this drink, pay attention to the smallest details, shake with care and energy all the ingredients in the shaker to obtain a consistent and plump froth, and do not forget to garnish with a few coffee beans.

~~~~~~

Godmother
It is part of the Mafia trilogy cocktails, together with the French Connection and the Godfather.

French Connection Story
The story around these 3 drinks dates back to the 50s, when the homonymous French criminal organization dominated the drug market, from France to the United States.

The ingredients are cognac (French spirit) and Amaretto di Saronno (Italian liquor) and as the heroin traffic was produced near Marseille by French and distributed throughout the United States by the Italo-American clan, in order to celebrate their victories, the criminals were drinking these dangerously delicious drinks.

As a cocktail is a classic after-dinner dessert or meditation, try it with or without ice, maybe even with some mature cheeses or even some cakes.

Ingredients
- 35 ml amaretto
- 35 ml vodka (replace vodka for whiskey and have a Godfather; replace vodka for cognac and have a French Connection).

How to make it

Stir the ingredients over ice and serve in an old-fashioned glass with or without ice.

Garnish

Normally there is no garnish but some essential oils from a citrus peel can help to improve the flavour of the drink.

French Martini

French Martini is one of the most pleasant cocktails you can mix and this is because of its delicate touch of the raspberry liqueur and the tropical touch of the pineapple juice, which is creating this symphony of aromas.

As a tribute

The French Martini can be drunk at any time but be careful because the alcohol content is quite high; you don't feel it because its pleasantness will invite you to drink it, especially if you serve well-chilled. It is believed to be invented in the late 1980s in a bar in New York as a tribute to the French liqueur Chambord (cognac base raspberry liqueur).

Ingredients

- 4 fresh raspberries
- 5 ml lemon juice
- 15 ml pineapple juice
- 15 ml raspberry liqueur
- 45 ml of vodka

How to make it

The cocktail is prepared in the shaker by adding all the ingredients and after a good shake, strain into a cocktail glass.

Garnish

Garnish with raspberries.

~~~~~~

Harvey Wallbanger

The Harvey Wallbanger is a fabulous drink by an elegant and refined taste, but never difficult.

Banging the head

The recipe is very simple, take a Screwdriver (vodka and orange juice) and add a dash of Galliano L'Autentico liqueur (golden herbal liqueur from Italy). The drink is reputed to have been invented in 1952 by three-time world champion mixologist Donato 'Duke' Antone and named after a surfer frequenting his bar in Los Angeles. The surfer was always drinking Screwdriver with a dash of Galliano L'Autentico and after won a surf competition he staggered from bar to bar banging his surfboard on the walls.

A competing story credited Bill Donner, host of a house party held in California, Newport Beach, and named after a guest was found banging his head the next morning complaining of the hangover that this drink induced.

Ingredients
- 50 ml vodka
- 100 ml orange juice
- 10 ml Galliano L'Autentico float

How to make
Part of the build-up family of drinks. Prepare in a tall glass over ice and remember the Galliano to be poured on top.

Garnish
Orange wedge.

~~~~~~

Moscow Mule

The Moscow Mule is considered a pillar of the history of cocktails.

The Mule from Moscow

The Moscow Mule is one of the most famous cocktails ever, it is a long drink with a not too high alcohol content. There are two stories regarding its birth:

One has John Martin of Gilbert F. Heublein, an American east coast spirits and food distributor based in Connecticut. He came out with this drink with his friend, 'Jack' Morgan, president of Cock'n'Bull Products -which was producing ginger beer, and the birthplace would be New York in 1941, after an evening meeting where they were enjoying this refreshing drink in some copper mugs representing a mule from Moscow.

The other story has Price, Morgan's head bartender, who created the drink when he needed to clean out the cellar full of unsold good stuff like Smirnoff vodka and ginger beer.

Ingredients
- 5ml lime juice
- 50 ml vodka
- 100 ml ginger beer

If you replace vodka with tequila the result is called El Burro or even Mexican Burro, Kentucky Mule is made with bourbon, and Gin Mule is obviously gin base. Use rum and you have Dark'n Stormy.

How to make
Part of the build-up family of drinks. Pour first the ice and then start with the ginger syrup and then the fresh lime juice. Add the vodka and complete with the ginger beer. Give a quick stir in order to mix all the ingredients.

Serve the Moscow Mule in copper cups (traditional way, on which a cute donkey was engraved), but also a simple highball glass fill with ice is fine too.

Garnish
Garnish with some ginger candies or go classic with a lime wedge.

Whisk(e)y cocktails

Whisk(e)y is a type of distilled alcoholic beverage made from fermented grain mash. Various grains – which can be malted – are used from different varieties including barley, corn, rye, and wheat. Whisk(e)y is typically aged in wooden casks, generally made of charred white oak.

The word whisk(e)y is an anglicisation of the Gaelic phrase *uisge beatha* meaning water of life (Latin is aqua vitae).

~~~~~~~~~~~~~~~~~~~~~~~~~~~~~~~~~~

Blood and Sand
Blood and Sand, a delicious drink by the blood-red colour is inspired by a historical film, with the legendary Rudolph Valentino as a toreador.

An Italian touch
If you want a refreshing drink, with a complex and suggestive taste, the Blood and Sand is an absolutely great choice. The recipe is well balanced and very precise: scotch, cherry brandy, sweet vermouth, and red-orange juice in equal parts. It first appeared in the 1930 edition of the unforgettable *Savoy Cocktail Book* and was named after 1922's *Blood and Sand*, a bullfighter movie starring Rudolph Valentino (Italian actor naturalized in the US).

Ingredients
- 20 ml blood orange juice
- 20 ml Cherry Heering (cherry liqueur)
- 20 ml sweet vermouth
- 20 ml scotch

How to make
When you use juices, you get a better taste when you use the fresh one, and this drink you will have a delightful result if use freshly squeezed blood orange juice.

Put all the ingredients in a shaker, shake and strain in a chilled cocktail glass.

Garnish
Garnish with an orange twist.

~~~~~~~~~~~~~~~~~~~~~~~~~~~~~~~~

Blue Blazer
This drink is more about the show than taste. I really suggest practising with water before doing this spectacular drink.

A spectacular serve
Preheat the tankards with boiling water and do the same for the balloon glass. Place the spirit in a tankard, ignite it, and start throw from one side to another. This is where the drink takes the name: from its blue blazer colour of the fire. Use the tankard to extinguish the fire.

This spectacular serve was created by Jerry 'The Professor' Thomas, know as well as the father of bartending and master of showmanship. He was working at the El Dorado gambling saloon in San Francisco when he developed his signature: The Blue Blazer. Legend has it that he would make the drink only if outside the temperature was 10°C/ 50°F or below, or if the person that ordered was suffering of cold or flu, so to be consumed as a medicinal remedy.

Ingredients
- water to warm glasses and tankard
- 3 dashes Angostura bitter
- Sugar to taste
- 100 ml scotch

Garnish
Orange twist and discard.

~~~~~~

Bobby Burns

This particular sweet and enveloping blend is a perfectly delicious drink, but what makes it so unique and drinkable?

"One of the very best whiskey cocktails"

Like many classic cocktails, they are numerous versions of the Bobby Burns but the one I like the most comes from *The Savoy Cocktail Book* by the legendary bartender Harry Craddock, from the first printed edition (1930), where Harry described this drink as "One of the very best whiskey cocktails."

It is named after Robert Burns (1759–1796), which is widely regarded as the national poet of Scotland and also a pioneer of the Romantic movement.

Ingredients
- 10 ml Dom Benedictine
- 25 ml sweet vermouth
- 45 ml scotch whisky

How to make
Put all the ingredients in a mixing glass filled with ice and give a stir. Stir and strain into a cocktail glass.

Garnish
Garnish with a lemon twist.

Try this: Buttered Bobby Burns using the fat washing technique.
Incorporating fat into this drink means that will add buttery flavour and lots of richness and creaminess sensation. Normally I use between 150 g to 250 g of fat products to 750 ml spirit.

The first thing consists of transforming the chosen fat into a liquid (if you are using oil there is no need for this operation) and combines it with the alcohol. Place in freezer overnight. Strain through a cheesecloth and ready to go.

Boulevardier

The Boulevardier is an elegant, intense cocktail, which makes of its simplicity a great pride.

Three simple magic ingredients

A few simple ingredients for a magical, fragrant blend, where the bitter taste of the bitter blends perfectly with the warm taste of the sweet vermouth and the great and complexity of the whiskey. Although the Boulevardier is one of the best cocktails as an aperitif, its alcohol content is quite high so be careful and don't exaggerate. This autumnal Negroni cousin creation is attributed to Erskine Gwynne, an American-born writer who founded a monthly magazine in Paris called *Boulevardier* which appeared from 1927 to 1932.

Ingredients
- 30 ml Campari bitter
- 30 ml sweet vermouth
- 30 ml whiskey bourbon

How to make
Part of the build-up family drinks but it can be also stirred. Serve in an old-fashioned glass with ice.

Garnish
Garnish with an orange peel.

Try this: Barrel-aged Boulevardier
Mix all ingredients in bigger proportion and add them into your barrel and aged them for as long you want in order to achieve your desire result and sample it often in order to avoid an over-aging product.

It is ideal if you previously 'washed' the barrel and I recommend using some fortified wine – port is a great candidate – but it is up to your imagination.

~~~~~~~~~~~~~~~~~~~~~~~~~~~~~~~~~~~~

Brooklyn
The Brooklyn is a pre-Prohibition classic drink and was largely forgotten until the recent cocktail renaissance. Now it is frequently found on drinks lists worldwide.

Where are you from?
The origins of the Brooklyn cocktail are not very clear, but it is certain that it was elaborated in the early 1900s; the first track of the Brooklyn dates back to 1910 when it was mentioned by Jacob Abraham Grohusko in his *Jack's Manual*, a booklet reprinted up to 1933.

In 1910, in a Nebraskan newspaper, the birth and paternity of the drink is entrusted to a certain Maurice Hageman, with a different recipe from that of today.

Ingredients
- 10 ml maraschino
- 10 ml Amer Picon
- 25 ml dry vermouth
- 45 ml rye

How to make it
Stir all the ingredients in a mixing glass and serve in a cold cocktail glass.

Garnish
Place a marasca cherry on the bottom of the glass.

~~~~~~~~~~~~~~~~~~~~~~~~~~~~~~

Irish Coffee
The Irish Coffee is one of the kings of hot drinks; what is its secret?

Irish Coffee is definitely a cup of pleasure
The drink was invented and named by Joe Sheridan, a head chef in Foynes, Ireland. He came up with this idea for a group of American passengers who disembarked from a flying boat due to miserable winter weather in 1940. He added whisky to a regular coffee to warm the passengers. They asked if they were drinking Brazilian coffee and Sheridan told them that it was 'Irish Coffee'.

Stanton Delaplane (famous travel writer from San Francisco Chronicle) brought Irish Coffee to the US and popularised it.

In practice, the Irish Coffee is a proper coffee with whiskey on which floats an irresistible layer of slightly whipped cream. And here lies the secret of the perfect Irish Coffee, the light shake that must be given to the cream to make it softer and airier, so that it does not sink into that black sea.

Ingredients
- 10ml brown sugar syrup
- 90 ml hot coffee
- 50 ml Irish whiskey
- Top double cream

How to make
In a thermo-glass pour the whiskey, the fresh-made coffee, the sugar, and stir and heat until is hot and all the sugar has dissolved completely.

Put the cream in the shaker and shake for 10 seconds, let it rest for a moment, and then pour it, slowly, into the glass, helping with the back of a spoon resting on the wall of the glass. You can aromatise the double cream according to your preferences. Garnish and serve.

Garnish
Garnish with freshly grated nutmeg.

Did you know...

- It is recommended to consume no more than 400 milligrams (mg) of caffeine a day.
- The average caffeine content of an 8-oz, brewed cup of coffee is 95 mg.
- A single espresso or espresso-based drink contains around 63 mg.
- Decaf coffee contains about 3 mg of caffeine (on average).
- Cold brew coffee contains approx. 100mg x 8 oz.
- Starbucks contains around 75mg per single espresso.

Manhattan
The Manhattan is one of the most famous cocktails in the world, a classic immortal, excellent as an aperitif, and is prepared with rye whiskey, vermouth, and a few drops of Angostura.

The legend that is not true
There was a chance that the drink was created at the Manhattan Club in New York. Even the Club's official history makes the claim. According to a popular legend, the recipe was created in 1874 for a party hold in honour of Jennie Jerome-Lady Randolph Churchill, Winston Churchill's

mother, but the drink expert David Wondrich in his Imbibe pointed that Lady Randolph was in England at that time to give birth to the little Winnie.

The other story which is more plausible is written by William Mulhall, a bartender at the Hoffman House. He wrote that a bartender called Black created this drink. This account comes decades after the drink appeared in the scene. The earliest record is found in *The Flowing Bowl* of 1891 by William Schmidt.

What vermouth do I use?

The ingredients for a Manhattan are:
- 3 dashes Angostura bitters
- 50 ml of rye
- **20 ml of vermouth:**
  - dry for a dry Manhattan and the garnish is a lemon twist.
  - sweet for a sweet Manhattan (which is the original recipe) and the garnish is a marasca cherry.
  - 10 ml sweet and 10 ml dry for a perfect Manhattan and the garnish will be an orange twist.

How to make it

In a mixing glass, over ice, add a few drops of Angostura and then pour the rye whiskey together with the vermouth.

Stir gently until the sides of the glass are moistened and almost freezing.

Serve straight up, garnish and serve.

The following are other variations on the classic Manhattan:

- Cuban Manhattan – a perfect Manhattan with rum instead of whiskey.
- Fanciulli – adds the bitter flavours of Fernet-Branca.

- The Fourth Regiment – a cocktail that uses equal parts whiskey and vermouth and uses three dashes of three different bitters – orange bitters, Peychaud's Bitters and celery bitters.
- Metropolitan – similar to a brandy Manhattan, but with a 3:1 ratio of brandy to vermouth and a dash of simple syrup.
- Rob Roy – made with Scotch whisky.

Mint Julep

The Mint Julep is a bourbon cocktail best known for being the signature drink of the Kentucky Derby. But this easy-to-make refresher shouldn't be reserved for only one day a year. This classic cocktail was created in the southern part of United States during the 18th century and is still a favourite worldwide today.

Medicinal benefits

The first news about Mint Julep dates back to the late 1700s, that it was consumed for medicinal benefits. It was common practice to prescribe Julep for anyone with stomach problems, digestive problems and nausea.

In the early years of its life, a Julep was based on rum and later also on brandy, but with the passing of time it became more and more American and whiskey replaced the rum and brandy. Mint Julep in the modern days is based on mint and bourbon-type whiskey with the addition of crushed ice. You can try also with your favourite spirit for new fantasies.

Ingredients
- 5 sprouts of mint
- 10 ml sugar syrup
- 60 ml bourbon whiskey

How to make

In an julep cup put the sugar and the mint. Muddle gently to extract the mint essential oils, then add the whiskey and fill with ice.

Garnish

Garnish with mint spring.

~~~~~~

New York Sour

Are you a wine and a whiskey lover but you can't decide what to have tonight? Just have both in this fantastic delicious cocktail: New York Sour.

What is your favourite wine?

The New York Sour is a classic 'whiskey sour' with the added boost of a dry red wine float. With the presence of egg white, you will have body and texture, and it will also help you to create the delightful drink's colour.

The choice of wine will determine the taste of the final drink: Tempranillo will offer plum notes and a black fruit character to the drink, Shiraz-cherry flavours.

The story of this cocktail goes back to the end of the 1800s and it was created in Chicago in the US.

Ingredients

- 25 ml lemon juice
- 12.5 ml sugar syrup
- 50 ml whiskey (bourbon)
- 15 ml egg white
- 15 ml red wine float

How to make

Shake the bourbon, lemon juice, sugar syrup and the egg white in a cocktail shaker with ice and strain the contents of the shaker into an ice-filled old-fashioned glass.

Float the red wine on the surface of the drink and serve.

Garnish
No garnish needed.

~~~~~~~~~~~~~~~~~~~
Old Fashioned
We are talking about one of the greatest and one of the oldest cocktails in the history of drinks, born towards the end of the 19th century, together with Sazerac, different for ingredients but with which it shares the same preparation, or it would be better to say, the same ritual.

How old is this fashion to mix whiskey, bitters and sugar?
Old Fashioned is a masterpiece with an intense flavour, enriched by the balsamic notes of the Angostura which are the background for the spicy taste of whiskey and the sweetness of the sugar.

The drink takes its name from the old-fashioned practice of 1800, which consisted of mixing the spirit with sugar and bitters. The glass used has taken its name from this cocktail.

In his 1862 *Bartender's Book or How to Mix Them*, Jerry Thomas listed a recipe for the Holland Old Fashioned Gin Cocktail and was made with genever rather than whiskey. Twenty years later, in 1880, at the Pendennis Club, James Pepper – bartender and bourbon aristocrat – was said to have invented the drink. Funny now but very useful back then, the Pendennis recipe calls for a slice of orange and cocktail cherries to be crushed in the preparation of the drink. It was done in order to mask the bad taste of the whiskey.

The same year, Samuel Tilden, 25th mayor of New York City and former Democrat candidate to be president of the USA held a party where sour mashes, hot whiskeys and Old Fashioneds were consumed. From here on this drink became famous.

Ingredients
- 4 dashes of Angostura bitter
- 10 ml sugar syrup
- 60 ml whiskey

How to make it
Stir all the ingredients together until ice cold and serve over ice.

Garnish
Garnish with an orange peel.

Try this: Old Fashioned syrup
The idea is to keep the soul of the drink intact, but our touch comes from the homemade Old Fashioned syrup: syrup based on elements that related to the original recipe: (sweet and bitter), mixed with the dark base spirit's flavours such as wood and chocolate plus the addition of citrus notes.

So, the syrup is based on:

2 parts water, 2 parts Angostura bitter, 1 part wood bitter, 1 part chocolate bitter, 1 part orange bitter. Heat this and add 2 parts of sugar (preferably demerara) for 1 part of the liquid, touch of salt and Arabic gum for silkiness.

All this means that this homemade will make you be more efficient, consistent, faster, innovative, plus will elevate the drink's profile.

~~~~~~~~~~~~~~~~~~~~~~~~~~~~~~~~~~~~

Rob Roy
Sometimes the simplest cocktails are the best. Rob Roy, part of the classics – the cocktails that have been around since the cocktail era – is still one of the top requested drink for a good reason: taste deliciously good!

The great operetta

The Rob Roy is a delightful cocktail and is essentially a Manhattan made with scotch. Like the Manhattan, the Rob Roy can be made 'sweet', 'dry' or 'perfect'. The standard Rob Roy is the sweet version, made with sweet vermouth, so there is no need to specify 'sweet' Rob Roy when ordering.

A 'dry' Rob Roy is made by replacing the sweet vermouth with dry vermouth. A 'perfect' Rob Roy is made with equal parts sweet and dry vermouth.

This fantastic cocktail was created in 1894 by a bartender at the Waldorf Astoria hotel in Manhattan, New York City and was named in honour of the premiere of Rob Roy, an operetta by composer Reginald De Koven and lyricist Harry B. Smith, loosely based upon Scottish folk hero Rob Roy MacGregor, know as well as Robin Hood.

You can try also a peaty whisky for a more intense result such as a whisky from Islay.

Ingredients
- 3 dashes Angostura bitters
- 20 ml sweet vermouth
- 50 ml scotch whisky

How to make
Stir the ingredients over ice and serve in a cocktail glass.

Garnish
Garnish with an orange twist.

~~~~~~

Rusty Nail

The Rusty Nail is another great drink that wins with its simplicity: scotch whisky mixed with Drambuie, a whisky liqueur flavoured with Highland herbs and honey.

The Rusty Nail is also excellent on its own, thanks to its perfect balance of flavours, but also try to accompany it with chocolate desserts or a soft orange soufflé or raspberry cheesecake and it will be a unique experience.

Symphony of flavours

The Rusty Nail is a classic after-dinner cocktail and offers a complex and mature symphony of flavours and aromas. The drink expert David Wondrich said that this drink first appeared in 1937 and is credited to F. Benniman and named after the British Industries Fair. Popularized in the 1950s at Club 21 in New York City, it takes its name from its colour, similar to a rusty nail.

Ingredients

- 20 ml Drambuie
- 50 ml scotch

How to make it

Stir the ingredients over ice in a mixing glass and serve in an old-fashioned glass on ice or without.

Garnish

I really like it with a lemon twist and discard.

Try this: Smoking Rusty Nail

Place the drink under a cloche and, using a smoking gun with hickory chips in the fire chamber, smoke your cocktail for few moments just enough to have some light notes of pleasant smoke before serving it.

Sazerac

The result of the ritual of making this exceptional cocktail is an enveloping and hypnotic drink, full of herbaceous notes that intertwine with the warm charm of cognac and the purple bitter of the Peychaud.

The magic drink

The Sazerac was born in the mid-1800s in the charming New Orleans, at the time a real Mecca for cocktails and alcohol pleasures. Many of the most famous cocktail recipes which are still appealing today were invented in this city, precisely in this period, thanks to a refined culture of drinking and the fact that the city was a crossroads of trade, especially whiskey, and meetings.

The drink is named for the Sazerac de Forge et Fils brand of cognac that served as its ingredient. With the arrival of phylloxera (an insect that caused serious damage to the production of cognac in the XIX century), the cognac had a frightening collapse and therefore the Americans astutely replaced the cognac with rye whiskey, and to say it all the result is still excellent today, perhaps less aromatic and floral, but more strong and dry as flavour.

In the beginning, the drink was used to be served in an egg cup, called *coquier* in French, and the story says that even the term cocktail derives from this word.

Ingredients

- 3 dashes Peychaud's bitter
- 10 ml sugar syrup
- 50 ml of cognac (can be made also with rye, or even half measure cognac and half rye)
- 10 ml of absinthe

How to make it
Put crushed ice in a glass, add the absinth and make sure to cover the walls of the glass perfectly. Stir the rest of the ingredients in a mixing glass and after you discard the ice and any excess from the absinth flavoured glass, pour and serve the drink there. Make sure to remove the absinthe, because it has a very strong flavour, otherwise the subtle balance of the cocktail is ruined.

Garnish
Garnish with a lemon twist.

Toronto
The Toronto cocktail is a variation of the Old Fashioned, with the addition of Fernet-Branca which gives the drink a minty and floral finish.

Nothing can stop us!
This is a richly flavoured, mildly bitter cocktail that is also perfect for the Fernet starters and it was first recorded as the Fernet Cocktail in Robert Vermeire's 1922 edition of *Cocktails: How to Mix Them*, in which he stated that the "cocktail is much appreciated by the Canadians of Toronto" – also because the importation of alcoholic beverages to Ontario was banned as a result of 1921 due to the Prohibition referendum, so they were using what was available then there.

Ingredients
- 2 dashes of Angostura bitter   - 10 ml Fernet Branca
- 10 ml sugar   - 50 ml Canadian whiskey

How to make it
Stir all the ingredients over ice in a mixing glass and serve in a cocktail glass.

Garnish
Orange twist and discard and marasca cherry.

Vieux Carré

Vieux Carré is a powerful, well-structured drink based on rye whiskey and cognac, but at the same time very mellow due to the notes of the sweet vermouth, complex and aromatic due to the presence of herbal liqueur Dom Benedictine and the presence of two bitters – Peychaud and Angostura.

Dating back to 1930

This great drink dates back to the 1930s, and it was created at the Carousel Bar at the Monteleone Hotel and takes its name from the eclectic Quarter of New Orleans which if translated means Old Square.

Ingredients
- 2 dashes of Angostura bitter
- 2 dashes Peychaud's bitter
- 10 ml Dom Benedictine
- 20 ml sweet vermouth
- 20 ml rye whiskey
- 20 ml cognac

How to make
Combine all the ingredients in a mixing glass filled with ice. Give a good stir and pour into an old-fashioned glass over ice.

Garnish
Garnish with some essential oils from an orange peel.

Whiskey Sour

The whiskey sour is an excellent drink, one of the easiest drinks to make, but also the one that has genuine taste, an essential elixir of beauty that has few rivals.

Before the egg white era

The history of Whiskey Sour is as old as whiskey itself since the method of preparation is that of the first cocktails: sugar in the glass, fresh juice, whiskey, and ice, or at least this is the first recipe written by the father of mixology, Jerry Thomas, in his book titled *How to Mix Drinks or The Bon-Vivant's Companion*.

Ingredients
- 25 ml of lemon juice
- 12.5 ml of sugar syrup
- 50 ml of bourbon whiskey
- 15 ml egg white

How to make it

It is prepared in the shaker. Add the fresh lemon juice, sugar and whiskey. Place lastly the egg white to avoid its eventually cooking and start by doing a dry shake (shake without ice) and then give a good shake with ice.

Serve in an old-fashioned glass on the rocks or even straight up.

Garnish

Use the essential oils from a lemon peel. As a personal touch I like to add few drops of aromatic bitter on top.

Rum and Cachaca cocktails

Rum it is distilled from sugar cane by-products such as molasses or directly from juice through a process of fermentation and distillation and this is a plant with very old roots, about 6000 BC. It is said that even the rum word derives from the scientific name of the plant: Saccharum.

The cachaça is the Brazilian distillate par excellence obtained by the distillation of sugarcane. The name cachaça derives precisely from the Portuguese *cagassa*, a term that indicates the white foam that is produced when squeezing sugar cane is produced on the surface.

Caipirinha
Caipirinha is the Brazilian national drink. It is an excellent drink for cooling off in the afternoon and can be enjoyed as an aperitif, after dinner, but also to serve throughout the meal especially with spicy dishes.

The natural remedy
There are many theories around how the drink was created, one of which suggests that a variation of the drink was used to help cure the Spanish Flu epidemic in the early 20th century. The original recipe likely contained garlic, honey, lime and other strong natural substances, a variation of which is still used to this day to help cure a common cold. And for the non-medicinal version, the balance of sweetness and acidity of the cocktail (plus the contrast of cold against the Brazilian heat) really set off the cocktail's flavour.

Ingredients
- 25 ml lime juice
- 12.5 ml sugar syrup
- 50 ml cachaça

How to make
Place all the ingredients in the shaker and add an ice scoop of crushed ice.

Shake 2 times and pour all content in old fashioned glass.

Garnish
Garnish with freshly grated lime.

~~~~~~

Cuba Libre

Cuba Libre is one of the easiest cocktails to prepare, with only three ingredients: rum, lime and cola.

For the freedom of Cuba

It is its story that is wrapped in mystery: believed to be created in 1896 to celebrate the freedom of Cuba, in a toast of the American Coca-Cola and the Cuban rum. But apparently Coca-Cola was first imported to Cuba in 1902, and some theories are suggesting that the original Cuba Libre could be probably Chanchancara – a drink made with aguardiente di cana, miel and limon – which can be translated to a Daiquiri.

For sure that the name of this cocktail derives from the shouts of joy of the inhabitants of Cuba, who took to the streets to celebrate the liberation of the island from Spain after a war fought alongside the United States.

Ingredients
- 50 ml rum
- 100 ml cola

How to make it
Part of the build-up family: prepare in a highball with ice.

Garnish
Garnish with a lime wedge and serve.

Try this: tepache instead cola
Tepache is a superb Mexican fermented drink with a low abv, rich in probiotics and antioxidants content.

Ingredients:
- 1 pineapple organic
- 1200ml filtered water
- 150 g panela sugar*
- 1 vanilla bark
- 1 star anise
- 1 cinnamon stick
- 3 cloves
- 3 green cardamom pods
- 1 g black pepper
- 3 g coriander seeds
- 2 g juniper berries

How to make it:
Rinse the pineapple, discard the top, the bottom and the core. Slice it and add a glass pitcher with the rest of the ingredients.

Give it a gentle stir and cover the container with a cheesecloth that will allow it to breathe and place into a dark and warm place where will ferment for 3–5 days. If you ferment for more than 5 days, you will move your pineapple beer into pineapple vinegar (which is delicious by the way).

Control it every day and remove the white foam that has formed on top of the liquid. When ready, strain and adjust if extra sugar is needed.

Bottle, label and refrigerate.

* If you don't have panela sugar you can substitute it with caster sugar, demerara, etc.

Daiquiri

On a hot, suffocating day, there is nothing better than a nice iced Daiquiri.

An American invention

Daiquiri, seductive cocktail, with a precise and clean taste and refreshed by the aromatic lime. It is an excellent aperitif but what are its origins?

Already the English sailors in the 1700s in order to fight scurvy were producing and drinking a potion called 'grog', strong and rich in vitamin C, which helped them during long crossings.

The legend that has more notoriety goes in 1905 when some American engineers working in a mine seems that invented it and gave it the name of a Cuban beach. It happened that the engineer Pagliuchi visited an iron mine in Cuba called Daiquiri, and here with the American engineer Jennings S. Cox, proposed at the end of the day to have a drink.

Legend has it that Cox had only rum, lime and sugar available. They mixed the ingredients in a shaker with ice and Pagliuchi said, "What's the name of this cocktail?" "It does not have a name... it could be a rum sour," Cox replied. Pagliuchi concluded: "This name is not worthy of a cocktail so fine and delicious as ours, we will call it Daiquiri."

Ingredients
- 25 ml lime juice
- 12.5 ml sugar syrup
- 50 ml rum (Bacardi has the trademark for this drink)

Change the sugar syrup for grenadine syrup and you will have a Bacardi cocktail.

How to make

Prepare in the shaker and serve in a cocktail glass.

Garnish

Squeeze the essential oils of a lime peel and discard.

~~~~~~

Dark 'n' Stormy

Dark 'n' Stormy is a really unique drink, one of the few in the world with its official license, which belongs to a company producing rum, born in Bermuda.

A royal practice

Dark 'n' Stormy is a perfect tasty cocktail for the hot summers. The key is the Gosling, a rich flavoured dark rum that plays with the freshness of ginger beer. The drink was created by the Gosling Brothers, in Bermuda, just after World War I, and come from a practice of the Royal Navy to mix their daily rum ratio with ginger beer to have a more decent drink.

Ingredients

- 50 ml dark rum Gosling
- 100 ml ginger beer

Squeeze some lime wedges if you like a bit sourer but consider that no Bermudian will add lime!

When using ginger ale instead of ginger beer and cognac instead rum you will end up having a Horse's Neck cocktail.

How to make

Fill a highball glass with ice, pour the dark rum and finish with the ginger beer in order to create this dark stormy effect.

~~~~~~

El Presidente

If you are a rum lover, but also you are enjoying the vermouth and you don't know what cocktail to have, El Presidente No 1 and No 2 are the perfect drinks for you.

Named after the president of...

The El Presidente earned its acclaim in Havana, Cuba, during the American Prohibition. There are actually two versions:

No 1 was created after a circa 1915 visit of the President of Cuba – General Mario Garcia Menocal y Deop – at the Seville-Biltmore hotel in the same country. The bartender who came out with the recipe is Eddie Woelke.

El Presidente No 1

- 3 dashes Angostura bitters
- 20 ml sweet vermouth
- 50 ml gold rum

No2 was named after president Gerardo Machado (1925).

El Presidente No 2

- 5 ml grenadine
- 20 ml white vermouth
- 20 ml curacao
- 45 ml rum blanco

How to make it

The drinks have in common the same technique, same glass and same garnish; Stir with ice, and strain into a cocktail glass. Garnish and serves.

Garnish

Garnish with an orange twist.

~~~~~~

Hemingway Special

The Papa Doble is nothing more than a Daiquiri in which the sugar is replaced with grapefruit juice and the famous liqueur made from the marasca cherries, maraschino.

No sugar, please

The drink was created by Costantino Ribalaigua Vert, the legendary head bartender of La Floridita in Havana, in Cuba, for Ernest Hemingway, after the great man said that the Daiquiri is a great drink, but he preferred without the sugar, following also the fact that he suffered from a hereditary diabetic disease. He asked as well for it to be made with a double rum ration. This drink became known as Papa Doble, taking the name from the fact that Hemingway was known as Papa there.

Later, another great bartender, Antonio Meilan, added maraschino and sugar to balance the sourness of the drink and make it more palatable.

Ingredients
- 10 ml lime
- 20 ml grapefruit juice
- 10 ml sugar syrup
- 10 ml maraschino
- 45 ml rum blanco

How to make it

Shake all ingredients. Strain in a cocktail glass and serve.

Garnish

Garnish with the essential oils from a grapefruit peel and use it as a garnish.

~~~~~~

Mai Tai

Mai Tai is another delicious and aromatic tiki cocktail and this is thanks to the aromatic taste of the almonds, the elegant tones of the rum, the citrus notes of the triple sec and the freshness of the fresh lime juice.

Out of this world

His name in the Tahitian language simply means good, because there is no need to add anything else. There are many recipes for Mai Tai: eleven and there are two rivals: Trader Vic's and Don the Beachcomber's.

The most popular recipe (see below) was created around 1944 by Trader Vic for his two friends from Tahiti: Ham and Carrie. After the first sip, Carrie exclaimed: "Mai tai roa aè" meaning that the drink is so good, that seems out of this world.

Ingredients
- 25 ml lime juice
- 10 ml orgeat
- 10 ml triple sec
- 20 ml dark rum
- 40 ml rum blanco

How to make

Put all the ingredients in a shaker with some ice. Shake until the mixture is ice cold and pour, filtering, into an old-fashioned glass or a tiki glass over crushed ice.

Garnish

Garnish with a lemon peel and mint spring.

~~~~~~

Mary Pickford

and... Action!!!

Another fantastic drink, named after the silent movie actress and wife of Douglas Fairbanks: Mary Pickford (1892–1979), during the time she was in Cuba filming a movie with Charlie Chaplin. It is said to have been created for her in the 1920s by either Eddie Woelke or Fred Kaufmann at the Hotel Nacional de Cuba while she was there.

Ingredients
- 5 ml lime juice
- 40 ml pineapple juice
- 10 ml grenadine syrup
- 10 ml maraschino
- 40 ml rum blanco (white rum)

How to make it
Add all the ingredients in a shaker. Shake well and serve in a cold cocktail glass, garnish and serve.

Garnish
Use a marasca cherry as a garnish.

~~~~~~~~~~~~~~~~~~~~~~~~~~~~~~~~~~~

Mojito
It is not just a cocktail, the Mojito is a Cuban symbol by very deep historical and very distant roots.

A Mojito a day keeps the doctor away
Mint was used around 1600 for its medicinal proprieties and especially to cure cholera during Sir Francis Drake's times.

Angel Martinez in 1950, at the Bodeguita del Medio popularized the drink but also the legendary Hemingway help to promote it. Very famous the phrase, "My mojito in La Bodeguita, My daiquiri in El Floridita."

Ingredients

- 7 mint leaves   - 50 ml rum blanco
- 25 ml lime   - Soda top up (approx. 45 ml)
- 12.5ml sugar syrup

How to make it

In a tall tumbler put the sugar and the lime juice. Mix carefully, add the mint, gently massage it with the muddler, add crushed ice, the rum and complete with a sprinkling of soda.

For Cuban recipe of the 'Mojito criollo', add a touch of Angostura bitter.

Garnish

As a garnish use mint sprig.

Piña Colada

Piña Colada it is always associated with the Caribbean's sun, white beaches and palms. But if you are too busy to go there just have this tropical drink and you'll be transported there in a sip.

Puerto Rico's official drink

The national drink of Puerto Rico since 1978, and literally means strained pineapple if translated, a reference to the freshly pressed and strained pineapple juice used in the drink's preparation.

Believe to be created by Ramon 'Monchito' Marrero at the Caribbe Hilton. He intended to capture the true nature of Puerto Rico and after 35 years serving the drink there, Puerto Rico rewarded him by proclaim his creation as official drink.

Ingredients

- 10 ml lime juice
- 90 ml pineapple juice
- 30 ml coconut cream
- 50 ml rum blanco

How to make it

Prepare in a shaker with ice but if you have a blender pour all ingredients and add three pineapple wedges plus four or five ice cubes and blend. You will have as a result this creamy, tropical drink perfect for the hot days and even when you miss the summer.

Garnish

As a garnish use dry pineapple and a cherry.

Planter's Punch

Part of the great family of the Caribbean drinks, by a preparation not simple, but the result is an excellent drink, if made well.

Believe to have originated at Planter's Hotel in Charleston, South Carolina, but the recipe originates in Jamaica.

Ingredients

- 25 ml lemon juice
- 35 ml orange juice
- 35 ml pineapple juice
- 10 ml sugar syrup
- 10 ml grenadine syrup
- 45 ml dark rum

How to make it

Place all the ingredients in a shaker full of ice and shake vigorously. Strain in a highball on ice and garnish.

Garnish

Garnish with mint spring and a marasca cherry.

Brandy cocktails

Brandy is an alcoholic beverage distilled from wine or a fermented fruit mash. The term used alone generally refers to the grape product; brandies made from the wines or fermented mashes of other fruits are commonly identified by the specific fruit name. Except for certain fruit types, brandies are usually aged.

Cognac has a world-renowned name and is one of the most popular distillates in the collective imagination when it comes to alcohol. In addition to being renowned as mediated distillate, cognac plays a very important role in mixing: just think of famous cocktails such as Alexander, Between the Sheets, Sazerac, Sidecar, Stinger, Champagne Cocktail, French Connection, just to mention few of them.

It is produced in the Charente, Charente Maritime and Dordogne regions and the name derives from the common French city of Cognac, which is attributed to the historical production of this brandy. It is in this area that is born and prospers on the vines that give birth to the wine that competes in the production of the famous cognac.

The production of this distillate is precise and disciplined by-laws, falling within the AOC (appellation of origin contrôlée).

Armagnac is a distilled wine spirit produced in the Armagnac region in Gascony in the southwest of France, from a blend of grapes that include ugni blanc, baco, folle blanche and colombard using column stills. The resulting spirit is then aged in oak barrels before release. In order to produce this excellent product, some important factors need to be taken in the general sense, especially the concept of the terroir. These include: geology, soil, climate, the grape variety, and the choices of the vine grower. Now it's time for a bit of story for a better understanding of this type of brandy.

Pisco
Aguardiente of the Andes, it has Peruvian-Chilean origins. It is obtained from the fermented must of some varieties of distilled grapes in the discontinuous copper alembic. Translated, it means 'flying bird' following its powerful effects.

It is reported that in the 19th century merchant ships loaded with merchandise that drove to El Callao did not start the voyage without having made a stop at Pisco to get an excellent aqua vitae produced in the region.

Calvados is brandy produced in the French region of Normandy, distilled from many different apple varieties (over 200 are legally permitted), and it is not uncommon to be over 100 different varieties used to make a single calvados. The combination of sweet, tart and inedible bitter apples is used to achieve the right balance of flavour.

~~~~~~

B and B
Absolutely a truly delicious drink that takes its name from the ingredients: equal parts of the seductive brandy, and the nectar liquor, Dom Benedictine.

The premix
Part of the classic cocktail family, even if is a bit forgotten, this drink wins with its simplicity in the ingredients but complexity in the taste.

It is often served on the rocks but also great straight up. Some drinkers prefer it slightly warmer (prep your snifter with warm water, dumping it before adding the spirits). It is almost always served in a brandy snifter and it makes an ideal after-dinner drink or nightcap.

This concoction was created around 1937 in New York at the 21 Club and it was so requested that it was even created bottles containing the premix of the two ingredients.

Obviously was sold as B and B.

Ingredients
- 35 ml brandy
- 35 ml Dom Benedictine

How to make
Part of the build-up family drinks but it can be also stirred or even warm up and serve hot. Serve in an old-fashioned glass with ice or a brandy snifter glass.

Garnish
I like to use some essential lemon oils.

~~~~~~~~~~~~~~~~~~~~~~~~~~~~~~~~

Brandy Alexander
The Brandy Alexander is a famous cocktail based on cream; one of the greatest after dinner drink ever.

Still a mystery
The Brandy Alexander is a cocktail that does not fear the seasons and if you feel adventurous, you can experiment the original Alexander recipe, made with gin, which is always very pleasant.

Regarding its birth nothing is known of certain: the fact that the original recipe foresaw the gin suggests that it came from England, but many believe it was invented by an elusive New York bartender named Alexander just before Prohibition broke out.

One of the first written recipes appears in the book by Hugo Ensslin, *Recipes for Mixed Drinks* (1915), although it is not mentioned with this name and later was changed the gin with brandy as is very famous these days the Brandy Alexander.

Ingredients
- 30 ml fresh cream
- 30 ml crème de cacao brown
- 30 ml brandy

How to make
Pour all the ingredients into the shake, shake and strain into a chilled cocktail glass. Garnish and serve.

Garnish
Garnish with freshly grated nutmeg on top.

~~~~~~

Brandy Crusta
The Brandy Crusta, part of the old school cocktails, is one of the few cocktails that you need to garnish before making the drink.

What is a crusta?
Born in New Orleans around 1850 from the inspiration of Joseph Santini, Brandy Crusta owes its name to the particular edging of sugar on the glass in which it is served, called Crusta and its garnish composed of lemon peel that almost completely covers the part inside of the glass.

Ingredients
- 3 dashes Angostura bitter
- 20 ml lemon juice
- 5 ml maraschino
- 10 ml triple sec
- 45 ml cognac

How to make it
First of all prepare the glass (flute) with a sugar rim: moisten the rim with a lemon edge and dip it into a saucer filled with caster sugar. Pour all the ingredients into a shaker filled with ice, shake then strain into the prepared glass.

Garnish

The original garnish is with a large spiral of lemon inside the glass and sugar rim. But if you dehydrate some lemon peel, turn into powder and mix with the sugar you have some amazing citrus flavoured sugar rim.

~~~~~~

Brandy Eggnog

The Brandy Eggnog is a rich, warm dairy-based drink, and with the presence of the yolk you will have a frothy texture, and the name. It is normally made with brandy, as the name suggest but you can even try with bourbon or even rum.

The debate

Throughout Canada and the United States, eggnog is traditionally consumed over Christmas season every year, from late November until the end of the holiday season. The Online Etymology Dictionary states that the term 'eggnog' is an American term introduced in 1775, consisting of the words 'egg' and 'nog', with 'nog' meaning 'strong ale'.

In Britain, the drink was originally popular among the aristocracy. "Milk, eggs, and sherry were foods of the wealthy, so eggnog was often used in toasts to prosperity and good health."

Ingredients
- 50 ml milk
- 10 ml sugar syrup
- 1 yolk egg
- 50 ml brandy

How to make it

Pour all the ingredients in a shaker and shake vigorously for a good amount of time. Pour, filtering, into a highball glass filled with ice.

Garnish

Add a sprinkle of nutmeg (or cinnamon) as a final touch and serve.

There are endless versions, and the drink can be prepared with whiskey, rum, sherry, marsala. If you want a velvety cocktail, substitute half of the milk with fresh cream and add a tuft of whipped cream on the surface of the cocktail.

Champagne Cocktail

The ritual to prepare this historic cocktail is simple and observing the bubbles that slowly fill the glass and explode in a foam full of perfumes makes the Champagne Cocktail one of those drinks that you fall in love simply by looking at it.

The cocktail competition

The Champagne Cocktail is an ideal drink for brunch, aperitifs and also celebrations.

Regarding this recipe, it is said that in 1889 an American journalist organised a cocktail competition between his colleagues in New York and a certain Mr. John Dougherty won with this recipe. This story is not so reliable because the cocktail would appear in some recipe books compiled long before the presumed date of birth: it would be in fact in the famous *The Bartender Guide* by Jerry Thomas of 1862, and probably also in the publication of the previous year, in 1861, of *Mrs. Beeton's Book of Household Management.*

Ingredients
- 1 sugar cube
- 3 dashes of Angostura
- 30 ml cognac
- top up with champagne

How to make

In a flute put the lump of sugar, flavour it with Angostura, pour the cognac and then fill it with champagne.

Garnish

The original recipe prescribes a lemon peel as a garnish, but now the use is very invaluable, so go for the essential oils from an orange peel. Discard.

~~~~~~

Champs-Elysees

From *The Savoy Cocktail Book*

Champs Elysees is a warm drink by an elegantly herbal finish and seems to have first appeared in the Harry Craddock's 1930 *Savoy Cocktail Book*. It is named after the famous French boulevard: Champs-Elysees.

Ingredients

- 3 dashes Angostura bitters
- 25 ml lemon juice
- 10 ml sugar syrup
- 15 ml Green Chartreuse
- 45 ml cognac

How to make it

Add all the ingredients in a shaker. Shake well and strain in a cold cocktail glass.

Garnish

Garnish with a lemon twist.

Corpse Reviver 1

The Corpse Reviver is not just a single drink; it is a cure to the hangover. Or at least this is the category that is part of.

The purpose

Of the many classic Corpse Reviver recipes, only No. 1 and No. 2 survived the test of time and according to *The Savoy Cocktail Book* (by Harry Craddock, 1930 edition). A Corpse Reviver is a drink that needs "To be taken before 11 a.m., or whenever steam and energy are needed."

The purpose of this miraculous cocktail was to 'awaken' the unfortunate drinkers from the previous night's hangover, a function once attributed to the famous Bloody Mary. They were in fact also called 'eye-openers', strong enough to perk up the senses, open the eyes, revive indeed.

Ingredients

- 20 ml sweet vermouth
- 20 ml calvados
- 45 ml brandy

How to make it

Add the ingredients into a mixing glass, stir well and strain into a cocktail glass.

Garnish

Serve with an orange twist.

East India Cocktail

The East India Cocktail is an excellent drink, one of the pre-prohibition drinks but in an improved style. Gets its popularity thanks to some ingredients that were very fashionable back in the days: the cognac, the maraschino, triple sec and the bitters.

Named after...

First mention of this drink comes from 1900 edition of Harry Johnson's *New and Improve Bartender's Manual*. Later he updated the recipe, making several alterations, replacing raspberry syrup with pineapple syrup and swapping Boker's bitters for Angostura. The original recipe requests only a lemon twist; in the second he gets creative, suggesting a "cherry or medium-sized olive."

Ingredients
- 3 dashes Angostura bitter
- 10 ml grenadine syrup
- 5 ml triple sec
- 5 ml maraschino
- 45 ml cognac

How to make it
Stir all the ingredients and strain in a cocktail glass. Garnish and serve.

Garnish
Garnish with a citrus twist to give some freshness to the drink.

Pisco Sour

It is an elegant and refreshing drink that awaits you before a meal but great also as an all-day cocktail, very fragrant and intense like the colours of this beautiful and ancient, but still so wild, south American land.

The story of an immigrant and his invention

The inventor of the Pisco Sour is Victor Morris, an immigrant from Salt Lake City, US, who arrived in Peru in 1913. After a first period spent working for the Cerro de Pasco Railroad, a railway company based in the heart of the Andes at 4380 metres above sea level, Victor moved to Lima and there, in the centre, opened the Morris Bar in 1916 and the venue soon became the meeting place of the Peruvian upper class and English-speaking foreigners. Morris, nicknamed 'El Gringo' – as often happened to many Westerners – tried to enhance the local distillate by creating a variation of Whiskey Sour. This exotic drink had a lot of success from the beginning. After the death of Victor Morris, in 1929, the Morris Bar closed its doors after 13 years of activity, but its Pisco Sour continued to spread throughout Lima until it became a national drink: every year on the first Saturday of February there is even a party that celebrates it.

Ingredients

- 25 ml of lime juice
- 12.5 ml of sugar syrup
- 50 ml pisco
- 15 ml egg white
- 3 dashes of Amargo Chuncho Bitter

How to make it
In a shaker put the lemon juice, sugar, pisco and lastly the egg white. Shake vigorously to whisk the egg white lightly and then add the ice and shake again. Serve straight up or on the rocks.

Garnish
Place the Peruvian Amaro over the foam as a garnish.

Try this:
Instead of egg white use 3 drops of soapbark, which is a bark extract. It is gluten-free, vegan-friendly, odourless, cheap and gives you a superb meringue-like foam.

Sidecar

One of the most popular cocktails since the period of American prohibition, due to its strong and persuasive character but also because easy to prepare and easier to drink.

A drink of a certain style

The recipe of this stylish drink does not provide great difficulties. All the sour is worth the advice to carefully calibrate with the sweet-acid contrast. So taste the lemon, which must be well ripe, and always filter the juice. If you want it sweeter, increase the dose of triple sec or add a rim of sugar.

Although not well known exactly, the Sidecar is said to have been invented by a barman named Harry MacElhone, founding father of Harry's Bar in Paris, when one evening a man broke down the window of the local by entering with his sidecar, asking the barman for something to drink.

Another story, the most historical one, says that the Sidecar cocktail was created in honour of an American captain in service during the Second World War who used to go to his favourite place by riding a sidecar.

Ingredients
- 25 ml lemon juice
- 25 ml triple sec
- 50 ml cognac

How to make
Pour all ingredients into a mixing glass filled with ice. Stir well and strain into a cocktail glass.

Garnish
Garnish with a sugar rim.

Try using grilled lemon juice to add layers of flavours by grilling the lemons and then squeezing the juice out of them.

~~~~~~~~~~~~~~~~~~~~~~~~~~~~~~~

Stinger
When you approach the nose to a glass containing this drink, a world opens up full of sweet and menthol fragrances that run after each other.

The mask
The Stinger is one of the most essential cocktails, based on only two ingredients: warm cognac and the refreshing touch of the crème de menthe.

The name Stinger literally means sting, a name given for certain drinks by the long refreshing and pungent mint flavour, and it is said that was born in the early 1900s and came to success during prohibition because the dominant flavour of the crème de menthe masked the poor taste of alcohol of that time.

Ingredients
- 20 ml crème de menthe green
- 50 ml cognac

How to prepare it
Put the ingredients in a mixing glass filled with ice and stir gently, but long enough to allow the crème de menthe to melt in the cognac. Pour into a chilled cocktail glass and serve.

Garnish
No garnish needed.

Tequila and mezcal cocktails

Tequila is not simply an agave spirit, to bear this name it must be produced in the Jalisco state in the following regions: Michocan, Colina, Guajanato, Meyorit, Jalisco, Amatian city and/or Tequila city.

It must be made with only blue weber type of agave and be produced under the supervision of the Tequila Regulatory Council, set up in 1994. Authentic tequila will carry also a Norma Oficial Mexicana, or NOM, is a number on its label that identifies the producing company and guarantee that the tequila is produced following specific regulation.

~~~~~~~~~~~~~~~~~~~~~~~~~~~

Margarita

Margarita is a very easy cocktail: tequila, triple sec and lime juice. It is one of the most popular cocktails and is found in every corner of the world.

I have an allergy...

It is perfect as an aperitif, thanks to its strong but balanced taste between the sweetness of the triple sec and the acidity of the lime. The 1937 *Caffe Royal Cocktail Book* contains a recipe for a cocktail called Picador using the equal proportions tequila-triple sec-lime.

There is another story that links the word 'daisy' with the Margarita and considering that translating 'daisy' in Spanish it means margarita.

But the story that I like the most is that Margarita was invented by Carlos Herrera at his restaurant Rancho la Sloria, for the customer and Ziegfeld dancer Marjorie King, who said she was allergic to all spirits but not to tequila.

Ingredients
- 25 ml fresh lime
- 25 ml triple sec
- 50 ml tequila

How to make it
Personally, I like to add 5 ml of agave to have a more balanced cocktail. Put all the ingredients together with ice in a shaker and give it a good shake. Double strain and serve straight up or on the rocks.

Garnish with salt rim. To execute, take a slice of lime and wet slightly half edge of the glass.

Dip the wet edge of the glass into the salt and shake to remove the excess of salt.

Try this: Pickle Mango juice for the Margarita
- 2 mangos cut into small pieces
- 250 ml mango juice
- 175ml champagne vinegar
- 175 g caster sugar
- 3 g salt
- 3 g black pepper
- 2 g bay leaves
- 3 g coriander seeds
- 1 g fennel seeds

Add all the ingredients and simmer for 20 minutes.

Strain and add a touch of alcohol to better preserve the mixture.

Paloma

The Paloma cocktail is a very fresh drink made from grapefruit soda and tequila, but if you can't find the grapefruit soda use freshly squeezed grapefruit juice and top with soda – and maybe a bit of agave for a better taste.

Little is known about the historical origin of the Paloma, one of the most popular tequila-based cocktails in Mexico. Regarding its birth some believe that it is named after 'La Paloma' ('The Dove'), a popular folk song composed in the early 1860s.

Ingredients
- 50 ml tequila
- top grapefruit soda

How to make
Build the drink in a highball

Garnish
Garnish with a grapefruit wedge.

Tequila Sunrise

With the wave of euphoria for fermented agave juice, delicious and joyful cocktails were created, and Tequila Sunrise is definitely one of them.

The delicious chromatic effect

The name refers to the main ingredient, tequila, and the bright colours of the cocktail that recall the sunrise, which is given by the orange juice and grenadine, and which slowly fall into the cocktail colouring, like the sky at dawn. Pay attention because its tasty flavour makes you lose sensibility.

167

This popular version was created in 1970 by Bobby Lozoff and Billy Rice in North California. Legend says that they spent an entire day and night at the bar sharing stories and when the sun rose, they were still enjoying this drink, so decided to name it after the sky's colours.

When the Rolling Stones were on tour in 1972, this became the favourite drink of Mick Jagger. Even the tour was known as 'Cocaine and Tequila Sunrise' Tour.

Ingredients
- 100 ml orange juice
- 50 ml tequila
- 10 ml grenadine

How to make
Pour the tequila into a highball full of ice cubes. Pour the orange juice, give a quick stir and then pour the grenadine syrup over, which will slowly slide towards the bottom, creating the chromatic effect that gives the name to the cocktail.

Garnish
Garnish with an orange slice.

Tommy's Margarita

In 2003 Julio Bermejo was appointed Ambassador of Tequila to the United States and nowadays he continues to promote tequila all over the world. He is also credited with the invention of one of the best-known and enjoyed cocktails in the world.

The family's restaurant
This exceptional drink was created in the early 1990s, by the tequila expert Julio Bermejo, as a variation of the iconic Margarita, and named after his family's Mexican restaurant and bar in San Francisco, the self-proclaimed 'Premier tequila bar on earth'.

Ingredients
- 25 ml lime juice
- 12.5 ml agave syrup
- 50 ml tequila

How to make
Prepare in a shaker with ice. Strain in an old-fashioned glass over ice and serve.

Garnish
No garnish needed for this drink.

Rosita
The origins of this drink are unknown, but it is thanks to the legendary bartender Gary 'Gaz' Regan, who discovered it in 1988, that we can enjoy it today.

Ingredients
- 2 dashes of Angostura bitter
- 15 ml sweet vermouth
- 15 ml dry vermouth
- 15 ml Campari bitter
- 40 ml tequila reposado

How to make it
Add all the ingredients to a mixing glass. Add the ice and stir.

Garnish
Serve the drink in a cocktail glass and garnish with a lemon twist.

Sparkling and other creamy cocktails

Champagne is a sparkling wine produced in the Champagne region in France, and to wear this name four basic rules must be respected:

- First of all, the grapes must come exclusively from the area of the Champagne region.
- The second rule refers to the grapes: Chardonnay, a white grape that gives finesse and elegance; Pinot Noir, a black grape that brings taste and strength; the Pinot Meunier, a black grape that gives freshness and longevity.
- The third rule requires winemaking scrupulously respectful of the rules codified by the law, the result of the experience gained over the centuries. Special mention goes to the fact that the secondary fermentation of the wine must be in bottle.
- Finally, the wine must be produced and bottled only in the area delimited also from different vintages, intending to create an appropriate product, even in less favourable years.

Prosecco is a wine that can be produced only in some areas of Veneto and Friuli Venezia Giulia (in the north of Italy), from Glera, Verdiso, Pinot white, grey or black grape variety and only with the Charmat method.

The base wine is placed in large pressure-tight steel containers, and yeasts and sugary substances are added. In this way, the refermentation is activated, which allows the formation of the much-loved bubbles and increases the alcohol content. This method, called the Charmat Method (or Martinotti Method), is rather quick and allows to obtain a sparkling wine in a few months.

Aperol Spritz

Excellent symbol of aperitif, from an old tradition, comes a drink known and appreciated worldwide: the Aperol Spritz.

The true origins

Spritz is an aperitif alcoholic drink that in the past was obtained thanks to the union between water and sparkling wine. Spritz was born during the Austrian domination in the Lombardy-Veneto region, in the north of Italy, between the end of the 18th century and the beginning of the 1800s. In fact, the Austrian soldiers spread this drink, adding to the Veneto wine, considered by them too strong, seltz to dilute it.

The Spritz name, which derives from the German verb 'spritzen' which means to spray. Spritz today is presented in many variations but the best known is the Aperol Spritz.

Ingredients

- 50 ml Aperol   - 90 ml prosecco   - 1 splash soda

How to make

Part of the build-up family drinks. Prepare over ice in a wine glass for the classic way. But the way I like it the most is in a highball glass.

Garnish

Garnish with an orange slice.

Bellini

The Bellini used to be the king of the summer, but with the availability of the peach puree all year, you don't need to wait for the summer to have this elegant and refreshing drink.

The owner's invention

Another great drink that wins with its simplicity, in fact, the key is in the two ingredients used: peach nectar that provides fragrant aromaticity and sparkling wine. that gives structure and minerality.

Bellini cocktail was born in Venice, at Harry's Bar, in 1948, by the hands of the head bartender and owner Giuseppe Cipriani, on the occasion of an important exhibition in honour of the famous painter Bellini.

Cipriani used this name for the drink because its unique pink colour reminded him of the toga of a saint in a painting by the 15th-century Venetian artist Giovanni Bellini.

Ingredients
- 50 ml white peach nectar
- 100 ml sparkling wine or champagne

How to make
The secret to a wonderfully delicious Bellini is the peaches, which must be white, well ripe, but above all crushed in a fine colander to obtain pure peach nectar.

First of all, wash and peel the peaches, cut into wedges and place them in a colander and with a spoon crushed to extract the nectar of peaches. Pour in a flute and gently complete with the wine.

Try also a Puccini, replacing the peach pure with mandarin juice, a Rossini, which uses strawberry pure, or a Tintoretto, which is made with pomegranate juice.

Try this: Add a touch of lacto fermented peach to your Bellini.

- Lacto fermented peach
- 375 ml water
- 12.5 g Himalayan salt

- 250 g peach
- 375 g Honey

How to make

Carve the peaches and remove the pits. Mix the rest of the ingredients and make sure to dissolve the salt. Place all the ingredients in a vacuum bag, remove the air and leave to ferment for 5 to 7 days at room temperature. After the fermentation period, slowly open the bag and strain the liquid. Bottle and refrigerate.

Buck's Fizz and Mimosa

Buck's Fizz and Mimosa are two cocktails that share the same ingredients: orange juice and champagne, the only thing that differentiates them are the doses.

Fizzy family

The Buck's Fizz is named after London's Buck's Club, where it was invented as an excuse to begin drinking early; it was first served in 1921 by a barman named Malachy McGarry. Traditionally, it is made by mixing two parts champagne and one part orange juice. Some older recipes list grenadine as an additional ingredient, but the International Bartenders Association recipe does not include it.

Four years later, the Mimosa cocktail was invented at the Hôtel Ritz Paris by Frank Meier, in about 1925. It is probably named after the common name in Europe for the yellow flowers of Acacia dealbata.

Buck's fizz

- 50 ml orange juice
- 100 ml champagne

Mimosa

- 75 ml orange juice
- 75 ml champagne

How to make
Part of the build-up family drinks. Prepare and serve in a flute.

Garnish
No garnish needed.

~~~~~~

Kir Royal
The Kir Royal is a very simple cocktail, its recipe is elementary, and you need only two ingredients: the flavour and the bubbles of the loved French sparkling wine and the sweetness of another French delicacy, a blackcurrant liqueur called crème de cassis.

The mayor Kir
The difference between Kir and Kir Royal is very simple, the Kir is made with dry white wine, while the Royal is the luxurious version prepared with champagne.

Named after Felix Kir, the mayor of the French region Dijon, which was offering this his invention in the aperitif style to all guests visiting the Dijon Town Hall.

Ingredients
- 15 ml crème de cassis
- top champagne

How to make
Part of the build-up family drinks. Pour first the blackcurrant liqueur and top up with the champagne (for the Kir Royal, make in a flute) or with dry white wine for the classic Kir (made in a wine glass).

Garnish
No garnish needed.

Golden Cadillac

Golden Cadillac, an unforgettable cocktail with a rich and velvety taste, dominated by the taste of the charming Italian liqueur, Galliano.

Very simple recipe: 3 ingredients present in equal parts: Galliano liqueur, white crème de cacao and fresh cream, and the result is a soft dream on which to lay your lips.

The luxurious car

The Golden Cadillac cocktail is a cocktail born in the United States in the early 60s in honour of the famous film *The Solid Gold Cadillac*, where the main protagonist was the legendary Cadillac Eldorado, one of the most luxurious and expensive cars of that time, the price of which reached an exorbitant figure almost surpassing that of Rolls Royce.

Ingredients
- 30 ml of fresh cream
- 30 ml Galliano L'Autentico liqueur
- 30 ml crème de cacao white

How to make it
Pour all the ingredients into a shaker. Shake well and strain into a chilled cocktail glass.

Garnish
Golden leaf.

Grassho,pper

It's a classic after-dinner cocktail, almost a dessert, immediately recognized for its intense green dress.

Frisky insect

The Grasshopper is a velvety delicious cocktail that will please your palate with its simplicity and freshness: its recipe is quite simple: two liqueurs (crème de menthe and crème de cacao) and cream.

It takes its name from the small, frisky insect: the grasshopper. In fact, around 1930 a London based barman observed in a meadow in Piccadilly Circus this nice jumping animal. He was inspired by the idea of creating a cocktail that had a chromatic resemblance to the small insect and the same characteristic of being energetic like a grasshopper. So he came out with this idea.

Ingredients
- 30 ml fresh cream
- 30 ml white crème de cacao
- 30 ml green crème de menthe

How to make
Pour the two crème and the cream into a shaker full of ice, close and shake vigorously, then strain and serve up.

Garnish
Garnish with a small mint spring.

Lightning Source UK Ltd.
Milton Keynes UK
UKHW020632161121
394010UK00008B/83

9 781913 962708